I am Not a Smartie Pants!

AMANDA THE BIZGAL
TELLS ALL!

All rights reserved. No part of this book may be used or reproduced in any manner whatsoever without prior written consent of the author, except as provided by the United States of America copyright law.

Limit of Liability/Disclaimer of Warranty: While the publisher and author have expended their best efforts in recounting the accuracy and events of this book, they make no representations or warranties with respect to the accuracy, applicability and completeness of the contents of this book. The advice, best tips and strategies contained within may not be suitable for the reader's situation, job search, entrepreneurial endeavor or career advancement. Neither the publisher nor author accepts liability of any kind for any losses or damages caused, or alleged to be caused, directly or indirectly, from using the information contained in this book. The publisher and author disclaim any warranties (expressed or implied),
merchantability, or fitness for any particular purpose.

Published by 22Ink, LLC, Milwaukee, Wisconsin
Cover Design by Jazzy, Edited by Jazzy
Author photos by John Grant
bizgal illustration by Nerissa Tutiven
Printed in the United States of America

Copyright © 2012 Amanda Guralski
All rights reserved.
ISBN: 0985496401
ISBN-13: 978-0-9854964-0-1

DEDICATION

To my family, friends and fans—thanks for your support and for always believing in me! Your confidence in me has been the power behind the bizMe brand!

WHAT'S INSIDE

Prologue

Chapter 1   1
Scared? Me too!

Chapter 2   9
Internships — career tryouts that fouled out

Chapter 3   15
Text me, call me, like me . . . bizMe!

Chapter 4   23
Creating the playbook — the bizplan

Chapter 5   30
Networking, smart schmoozing and working the room — bizgal style!

Chapter 6   37
Picture them in their underwear?

Chapter 7   45
Putting a price tag on you

Chapter 8   50
Savvy Social Media

Chapter 9   57
Being a TV Celebrity Branding Expert *is* Reality TV

WHAT'S INSIDE (CONTINUED)

Chapter 10 — 64
I always wanted a crown

Chapter 11 — 69
Toughen Up . . . thick skin is in!

Chapter 12 — 75
LEAP Day . . . is Every Day

Chapter 13 — 81
VIP Shout Outs!

And finally — 110

Amanda the bizgal career store — 111

> Thanks for supporting me in this awesome adventure as the bizgal! I'm lovin' it!
> xoxo
> Amanda

Prologue

Poised, Polished and Passionate is hardly the only way to describe Amanda the bizgal.

Always known as "G" she was the college and high school sports standout—number 22 with the ribbon in her hair as she pounded the volleyball, threw the javelin within centimeters of a record, sunk clutch free throws or scooped up grounders at third. Amanda the bizgal is a fierce competitor and wholeheartedly trusts the philosophy of Aristotle "we are what we repeatedly do. Excellence, then, is not an act, but a habit." She demonstrated this conviction early in life as she fervently tackled the perfect timing of tosses and spins to become a national baton-twirling champion at the age of 6. This drive to outplay, outperform, and outsmart continued as she earned the sought-after recognition of a D1 volleyball athlete by age 18 to her current recognition as author, national speaker, publisher, consultant, regular co-host of a local morning show, and celebrity and professional athlete career and branding coach. And all of this was accomplished by fueling her own fire, by creating her own entrepreneurial entity. Amanda the bizgal has never taken to being told she cannot do something, in fact it kindles her obsession to challenge herself that much harder. She has leveraged her competitive edge, her fascination for goal setting and her passion for life to discover the secret to getting what you want . . . hard work.

From her teammates to her clients, one thing is for certain when meeting Amanda—her personality is contagious and she radiates a passion for everything she does leaving you feeling that anything is possible.

Chapter 1
Scared? Me too!

I always giggle when I think about how some folks romanticize the birth of entrepreneurs—that in the delivery room, the sky opens up, a ray of sunshine beams down and angels sing as the doctor proclaims . . . we got another entrepreneur! I can promise you that did not happen to me! Quite the contrary actually . . . when I was little, enterprising thoughts were not top of mind. The outdoors was my domain—I was running around with all the boys playing hoops, riding bikes, and practicing the baton or setting the volleyball against the garage. I was not thinking about how to make money. I was thinking about how much better at sports I was than these boys. If you had your own lemonade stand, cut your neighbor's lawn, or babysat, you had more of an entrepreneurial spirit than I did. My love for competition began as a six-year-old when I learned very quickly that going after your dreams can be accomplished by practicing, hard work, discipline, fundamentals, applying criticism and believing in yourself more than anyone else. My mom really set the foundation for my success. She would watch me practice the baton for hours, pushing me to get better, perfecting my blind catches and neck rolls and making sure that I was paying attention to the details. Twirling is super competitive—think hours of practice to perfect a spin or elbow roll or flashy blind catch—and then think leg lines and tight spins and high kicks—twirling is skating, gymnastics, pageantry all in one physically demanding sport. Individual twirling competitors are absolutely amazing—and the twirlers from the South, East Coast and California were tough competitors. A part of every twirling competition is the interview—with questions ranging from the current political climate to personal aspirations to global topics. Every chance my mom had, she would casually interject an interview question into our conversations. She would never let me get away with conversation string-alongs such as 'like' or 'um,' not looking people in the eye when chatting, not standing or sitting up straight or not articulating what I wanted. Baton twirling is more than the cheesy parade routines; it's a sport that combines poise, precision, timing, discipline and amazing coordination skills.

Twirling was actually my first introduction to the concept of who challenges herself to be the best and who gets by with limited practice. I could tell the difference even at an early age. Twirling is one of the best all-around character-building and challenging programs to participate in when young and impressionable. One of my best individual moments happened when I was 6—first runner-up to Beginner Little Miss Majorette of America. As I progressed I won many trophies and always considered each trophy another step in the encouragement ladder—try harder, practice more, be the best.

So what happened? I twirled baton for 18 years and competed in hundreds of baton competitions all across the country not only as an individual but also as a corps member with the best baton corps ever-- The Daley Debutantes Baton and Drum Corps. I can never thank the founders of the Daley Debs for all the inspiration and drive that they instilled in me. This was my beginning of countless hours of teamwork—sweating together during long hours of practice in a 90 degree gym, huddling together to say the Corps prayer before competing against the Canadian and USA Corps, screaming together when victory was ours. This was my heartbeat—competition! There is nothing that compares to the feeling of hearing "Corps Ten-Hut" and beginning our incredibly high performance 4-minute routine. I have been a national champion for most of those 18 years but what twirling and my mom really taught me at age 6 is that anything is achievable with hard work, goal setting and determination.

Fifth grade rocked my world when I was introduced to volleyball, basketball and softball. Again, a goal was set as the sparkly sequined twirling costumes were now sharing closet space with blue and gold team uniforms. One season of fifth-grade volleyball and I march up to my parents and tell them "I am getting a full ride someday to play volleyball!" As crazy as this sounds coming from a 10-year-old, they believed that I could do it. My parents gave me the support I needed by giving me the opportunity to play Junior Olympic volleyball. I remember playing high school basketball games on Friday nights and then my dad driving me after the game to play club volleyball the rest of the weekend in Minneapolis, Indianapolis or Louisville — each a drive of five to seven hours. Playing competitive volleyball at this level is an opportunity that most people dream of and I was lucky to have these experiences at such a young age.

Coaching is everything and I have been blessed with amazing coaches that challenged me every day to push beyond what I thought was possible. I have had coaches in my face telling me what I have done wrong, throwing clipboards at me for a missed block, letting me spend time on the bench to refocus and coaches telling me that I will never get a full ride, but that never once stopped me from going after my goal. I knew what I had to do to be the best and I did it.

But let's fast-forward through thousands of volleyball games, a bronze medal at the Junior Olympics and many people telling me that a full ride for me was never going to happen. On February 2, 2000 I signed my letter of intent to Villanova University for a D1 full ride volleyball scholarship. I remember this day like it was yesterday . . . the phone call with the head coach at Villanova offering me a scholarship. I remember screaming for joy, it was such a cool moment. To see everything I had worked for come together was an awesome feeling. Everyone deserves to have a life experience like this.

After receiving the summer workout plan from the Villanova volleyball coach, I could not wait to get started. I followed that plan to a "T," never skipping a day or even an exercise, because when I arrived in August the team was up against a fitness challenge and there was no way I was not going to pass. If I had to guess how many hours I spent working out, it would probably total over 20 hours a week. Working out was truly all I did in between playing volleyball, twirling the baton and completing this fitness program. Just like when I was younger, my mom was right there with me timing my sprints, counting my laps and pushing me just one more mile. The crazy thing was that during that entire summer I had a crazy case of mono. Even though I dropped down to 100 pounds, I never missed a day of working out.

I arrive at Villanova a whole 100 pounds and blow through the fitness program including squatting the 200 pounds required without even blinking. It felt amazing to be a freshman coming in to play D1 volleyball and showing up almost everyone on the team . . . wait, what? . . . showing up everyone on the team??? I remember being in the locker room and talking to the veterans on the team and learning that same of them did not take the summer fitness program seriously and they were almost making fun of me because I did! Was I missing something? . . . This was Big East volleyball, one of the most competitive divisions of collegiate volleyball. Seriously, we were playing Notre Dame, UConn, Syracuse, Pitt, Seton Hall, Rutgers, Georgetown and Boston College. How are you not taking a fitness program seriously? Well our lack of seriousness to get into shape definitely affected the way we played volleyball. Our record was horrendous; I believe we were 9-27 for the season. My life had turned into sitting in airports, playing volleyball for 45 minutes because everyone beat us very quickly, and then sitting in airports again. I had been at college for three months and still had not met any friends outside of the volleyball team.

After several months of managing the lifestyle of a D1 athlete—practice, practice, travel, full load of classes, practice, practice, games—the hard-core realization smacked me in the face that I had no idea who I was besides an athlete. I had no other outside passions, no friends besides teammates, no life outside of gyms, weight rooms, and the locker room. The label "athlete" represents much more than just a fan base; it is a lifestyle, a personality, an identity, and for an athlete the word encompasses everything that we know. Our lives have been structured with passion, motivation, setting goals, coaching, accomplishment and never letting any injury or emotion hold us back from getting what we want. Although I loved the Wildcat identity at Villanova, I wanted to be in an environment where I could play competitive sports but also find my "career sport" that ignited the same passion for my future as volleyball had taken me so far. I wanted the feeling that I felt for volleyball to be a feeling I felt for the rest of my life. As awesome as it was to be a D1 athlete, I wanted to create an environment for myself that gave me an opportunity to find who Amanda was, outside the number 22.

After one semester I transferred to the University of St. Thomas in St. Paul, MN, where I played volleyball, softball and threw the javelin. It was such a better fit for me. I was able to remain very competitive in sports but also develop who I was beyond being an athlete. People always ask me how I could walk away from a full-ride playing volleyball at Villanova and transfer to a D-3 school. It wasn't an easy decision. I loved my team, the campus and being identified as a D1 athlete. Do I think back on my life and wonder what I would be doing, where I would be living, who I would be as a person and if my life would be as awesome as it is now? . . . Absolutely! But, do I regret leaving? . . . NO!

A change of cities from Philly to St. Paul did not magically produce clearer thinking. I had no idea or direction for my future. Even though I had always been a goal setter, when it came to long-term career goals, I came up empty handed.

My 10 best reasons why athletic training and sport participation can shape your life:

1. Discipline and self-control are valued commodities
2. Practice will make perfect in everything you do
3. Fundamentals lay the groundwork for the structure of life
4. Mental toughness is the key to success
5. Learning the difference between taking things personally and listening with an open mind and willing attitude
6. Applying criticism because it makes you better
7. Anything is possible when you challenge yourself

8. Your biggest competition is you
9. Never let people get in your head, it makes you unfocused
10. You miss all of the shots you don't take . . . recognize opportunity, embrace the challenge, understand that failure can be fleeting as long as "you keep your eyes set on the prize!"

My 10 best reasons why you might not want to walk away from a full-ride:

1. FREE education
2. Cafeteria smorgasbord — as much as you want, when you want!
3. The identity of being an athlete on campus is indescribable
4. Sporting really cool Villanova gear
5. Access to top trainers and medical staff
6. I think my parents probably would have bought me a car or a puppy, maybe
7. Special privileges on the road and on campus
8. Invites to awesome house parties
9. Big East Conference — playing at Georgetown, Notre Dame, Boston College
10. Did I mention four years of free education at a prestigious University?

Chapter 2
Internships ~ career tryouts that fouled out

If I mention the word "internship," what immediately comes to mind? Probably unpleasant and unflattering thoughts like unpaid, hours spent filing, faxing and photocopying, being treated like you're a nothing or an errand runner, and a big waste of time if you don't know what you want to be, right? It is not surprising to me when my soon-to-be college graduate clients, who have absolutely nothing on their resume, are unsure about their career direction. I ask them, "What have you been doing besides partying for the last four years?" I have yet to hear a credible answer as to why they have not made time for an internship. I even had a client tell me that the economy was so bad that companies wouldn't hire him even though he wanted to work for free! I strongly believe in the power of internships and I am going to show you why.

Like most students entering college, you may have no idea what you truly want to be, what to study or even what inspires your passion, so you start taking your pre-reqs hoping that one of these classes will spark a profitable and heartfelt future. I was no different. When I began at Villanova, freshmen were to select a school to enter like the school of Commerce and Finance. I thought business might be a good path for me, perhaps working for an ad agency someday, but truthfully, I had no idea. Even after transferring to the University of St. Thomas, I still did not know what I wanted to be. No class that I was taking at the time really interested me except one—marketing. I liked the idea of branding companies and coming up with cool ideas to bring products to market. I knew I wanted to continue my love for sports but wasn't sure how to mix the two . . . and there it was, the perfect resolution for my future—sports marketing. Once I considered sports marketing as a viable career choice, I became so excited to get started to see whether I liked it. I immediately thought of doing an internship for a sports team because what better way to figure out if you liked something than to actually do it.

Would you ever buy a car without test-driving it first? Would you purchase a house without walking through it? Why would you enter an industry without giving that career a test run, a preliminary tryout? Internships allow you to "test drive" different careers until you find the perfect fit.

I am not the type of person that sits around and hopes that a sports team in MN knows that a college girl from St. Thomas wants to work for them so, how will I make this happen? I picked up the phone and started dialing! Yes, cold calling for an internship that I had no idea if it even existed but it didn't matter to me. I started by calling the Timberwolves, the Twins, the Wild and then finally the Minnesota Thunder, an outdoor soccer team. I was hired almost immediately for a position that didn't exist to be the Marketing Coordinator for the MN Thunder. The reason why I am telling you this is because sometimes picking up the phone and creating something for yourself goes a long way. The Thunder wanted to hire an intern but didn't have the time to put the position together so I created the entire position. Working for the Thunder was an awesome experience because I learned first-hand how a sports team operates, how to deal with the egos of professional athletes and most importantly I found out that I definitely didn't want to go into sports marketing! I had no idea that not only do you work all day but also on game days you have to stay until after that game which was sometimes midnight! Who wants to do that?

On Amanda's list of career choices . . . cross sports marketing off the list!

Next up for me was my other motivator, MONEY! Everyone loves money and to a make a lot of it, becoming a financial advisor might put you right in the hot mix of revenue secrets and investment strategies. This was my thought process back in college. So I picked up the phone again and started calling financial institutions to see if they were looking for an intern. Once again I was successful because Piper Jaffray hired me as their marketing intern for one of their top female producers. My internship was UNPAID and my job was to coordinate a women's luncheon once a month by sending out invites, taking RSVP's, creating and printing name tags, ordering food and booking the speaker. Not all that exciting in terms of internships but I knew that I was positioning myself to meet some powerful women around the Minneapolis area . . . which I did! This internship, just as the MN Thunder internship, provided the opportunity to attain real world experience and the chance to give these careers a test run. I realized, just like before, that I had no interest in being a financial advisor. The financial world is not the best idea for someone intimidated by the world of mathematics and I was thankful to find that out during this internship rather than after I got my first job as a financial advisor and lost my client's money!!

My internships opened my eyes to careers that I thought I would love. These career tryouts afforded me the opportunity to test drive different careers at no risk. I got the experience of working for a small business as well as a corporation. I was able to see first-hand the corporate culture and how to navigate it. I also started to build my network of professionals who were instrumental in helping me become who I am today and have proven to be tremendous mentors on my career path.

My 5 best tips for why an internship should be on your resume:

1. **Real World Experience:** You might have an idea of how the corporate world is structured, but you are most likely misinformed. Internships are the best stepping stone to finding out the company culture that best suits your work style—large corporation, small business or a start-up. If you don't give yourself an opportunity to learn, how will you know which you prefer?

2. **Crossing off career possibilities:** Wouldn't it be awesome if we could try out every career we ever wanted? Regardless of how glamorous or adventurous or income producing a career may seem to our imaginations, every career has its mundane moments and develops a routine of regularity. No one pushes the panic button on how many internships you have had, but employers do look for a pattern of instability if you job hop because you can't find the perfect fit.

3. **Building your network:** It's all about whom you know and who knows you. Networking gives you the opportunity to meet professionals that already have a well-developed network that can make your job search so much easier. Your network begins to work for you and that community may help you land that first job.

4. **Unpaid internships can be better than paid:** Never pass up an opportunity to intern because there is no paycheck. As an unpaid internship is not a budgeted expense for any department, the opportunity exists to try out different career experiences within the same company. During my unpaid internship with Piper Jaffray, I was the marketing intern, but I was also able to work with the financial advisors to determine whether I preferred that aspect of Piper Jaffray services. If my internship was paid and the money was budgeted out of one department, I never would have had the opportunity to crossover and work within multiple divisions.

5. **It could turn into a full-time position:** The last internship that I had during my senior year turned into a full time position. I was one of the lucky graduates to have a job before graduation. Because they knew my work ethic and enjoyed working with me, I was able to negotiate my summer off and start in September! You never know what can happen but if you don't put yourself in an opportunity to be successful, I can promise you . . . nothing will happen!

Chapter 3
Text me, call me, like me . . . bizMe!

My turning point was second semester junior year sitting in a magazine writing class at the University of St. Thomas in Minneapolis. I began to develop the same feelings I had for sports and athleticism—a give-it-your all attitude was now growing for magazine publishing. My focus had always been athletics so paging through magazines wasn't really something I spent time doing. But as I started analyzing magazines and researching the journalistic structure of a variety of publications, I quickly became obsessed with the ads, the four-color glossy pages that would take me away to a world full of Gucci and Prada. I didn't want to be as skinny as the models in the magazine but I wanted to help create the lifestyle that the models portrayed. I loved the way the ads and images made me feel, so I decided I would be the publisher of Vogue or InStyle someday . . . very ambitious, I know but hey . . . I am a big dreamer.

I was so excited that I had finally figured out what I wanted to do for the rest of my life and, again I was anxious to get started. As I shared my career idea with all my friends our conversations always went back to how totally unprepared we felt to leave college and how terrified we were to find a job. We realized that the safety net of college would no longer be with us and we were not ready to part with the comfort and guidance of our professors. I started to really think about why we all felt this way and what we could do about it. This was during the season that the very first Apprentice came out. In that season everyone was 30 years old and younger, in the top 2% of their industry and they all shared this business savvy that made anyone watching the show jealous. I could not get enough of this show because I realized that I wanted to be one of them. I wanted to come into a company and rock it out the way the Apprentice contestants did. (A little fun fact—I tried out for the 2nd season of the Apprentice in Chicago and Bill Ransic, the first season winner, interviewed me . . . AWESOME!)

I took a step back and realized that even though I wanted to be the publisher of a major national magazine, I was just as terrified as my friends. There had to be resources available that catered to young professionals who were making the transition from college to the working world that discussed everything we needed to know in order to be successful in our careers. So I began researching online and through my college and public libraries and did not find anything that catered specifically to my generation and those behind me. The next logical step . . . well, if there is nothing out there to help the second largest generation next to the Baby Boomers, I will create it!! Sounds easy enough, right?

I knew I had the book smarts to be successful but I was not confident in my business 'street smarts' to achieve the success I envisioned. That's when the little dark cloud lingering over my head burst with inspiration and tada! the idea to create an online resource that catered to that transitional period between college ideology and the realities of the working world developed.

I spent my entire senior year researching this idea, talking with professors, and discussing it with all my friends and other students. "If I created a magazine that coaches and mentors the young professional on everything there is to know regarding your career . . . would you read it?" This is the question I asked over and over again.

Once again, an internship unwittingly paved the way for me. At the time of this evolution from nervous student to career gal with an idea, I was the marketing intern for Piper Jaffray. I talked to my boss about the idea I had to start my own magazine. She told me that one of the ladies in the networking group was the publisher of a small media company and they were getting ready to launch a new magazine. How sweet would it be to work for someone that was launching a new magazine so that I could learn how it was done right from the get-go? SOLD!

I introduced myself to the publisher and I soon became her intern and was given a full-time position after graduating. This was such an awesome experience for me because I helped with branding the magazine, naming it and developing a sales campaign. It also gave me an opportunity to practice selling a product that didn't exist yet which was exactly what I would have to do with my own publication someday.

Every year Minneapolis offers this incredible Magazine Day that is every girl's dream! The biggest thrill is opening the door to a room filled with every magazine imaginable, free for the taking! I begged the publisher to let the sales reps attend and she said yes. This was probably one of the best days of my life. I walked out of there with well over 100 magazines. Not only was it amazing that I could grab all these magazines, but the people that I met were outstanding and knowledgeable and became the beginning of my network. I met this wonderful woman who had started many magazines herself and for several publishing houses. So if there was anyone who was a veteran on launching magazines, it was this woman. I introduced myself to her, asked her if I could take her out for coffee and run an idea past her. She was hooked immediately. This woman was so influential to the making of bizMe—she taught me everything I needed to know from what to research, to creating surveys that worked, to the magazine design and everything in between.

In our entire year together, she never once did the work for me. She guided me along the correct path but I did everything on my own and I am so thankful for this. Having influential mentors in your life that offer guidance and challenge your thinking are gifts from God. bizMe would not exist if it wasn't for me taking a chance and introducing myself to her. I learned so much from her that I will treasure for the rest of my life.

If you are sitting around waiting for an idea to hit you like a lightning bolt, it just isn't going to happen. The best way to start thinking of ideas is to take a step back, look around to what is happening right in front of you or what is bothering you and ask yourself "how can I make it better?" That is how ideas become dreams that YOU make happen!!

My 5 best tips for making a dream a reality:

1. **Pay attention:** Ideas are generated by listening to conversations happening around you, observing body language, and paying attention to interactions, reactions, and group dynamics. What are people struggling with? What are the day-to-day frustrations that people find stressful? How can you fill that need and make life easier?

2. **It has to be a passion:** Don't start something for the sake of starting something because you will lose your fire real fast. This idea has to keep you up at night, the type of idea that

constantly preoccupies your thoughts. How will you know if it's your passion? You'll know by your actions — you doodle logos on cocktail napkins, your daydreams are not romanticized versions but visualizations of you as business owner, your new addiction is researching and planning rather than growing digital cities or reading newsfeeds, or even when seemingly engaged with those around you your thoughts drift you away to your business idea. That's a passion, not a whim.

3. **Put the idea out there:** Start having conversations about your initial idea, it doesn't have to be perfect but you have to find out if there is a need for your idea. Many of the best ideas thrive on uncertainty because you exude the confidence that your idea, innovation, solution is a winner. Best way to evolve is to start talking.

4. **Don't let negativity stop you:** I have had my fair share of haters for many of my ideas but it is up to me if I am going to believe them or push forward. People will always criticize; there is no escaping that. Don't let it affect you, easy as that. Apply the criticism, regain your enthusiasm, regroup, reorganize, and keep talking.

5. **YOU make ideas happen:** I cannot stress this enough. People like to make excuses of why some people can do it and others cannot. Stop making excuses. Go after it, take a risk and give it 200 percent.

bizME covers
June '07
Fall '08

Page | 22

Chapter 4
Creating the playbook: the bizplan

I was so green, so unaware, so much a rookie when it came to starting up a business venture. The idea of building a business plan was incredibly overwhelming and I had absolutely zero background knowledge on even where to begin or what to include. I believe that the majority of young entrepreneurs have a great idea that they want to share with the world and all of their energy is focused on getting that idea to the market. Details like financing, competitors, management structure, and identifying the demographic in minute detail are probably not the first considerations. But these are the essentials that have to gain the spotlight in order to conceptualize the big picture.

The web has lots of model business plans but finding a plan that fit my style and my idea was impossible. Think of a business plan as a narrative on accomplishments — it's the crystal ball of organizing your idea and anticipating or foretelling what the future holds. So no shamrocks, tarot cards or lucky dice will produce the fortitude needed to advance your business venture — it takes research, soul searching, talking with field experts and a plan. A plan that anticipates growth potential and financial resources in five year spurts. Lofty goals are tremendous but getting from A to B remains the logistic addiction that entrepreneurs thrive on. It's the uncertainty that keeps us motivated, that fuels our creativity, and sparks our energy to jumpstart our business plan into the updated version of the frying pan — the hot mess of reality.

I started at the beginning. I literally wrote down every idea I had for the magazine layout, content, my projections of how fast we were going to grow, the amount of money we would need to fund it, how much money we would make in the next several years and if this idea was even a viable venture. The key word to all of this planning is projection! I spent hours at the St. Thomas library researching publications, patent and copyright issues, types of ownership and the LLC vs. anything else. I discussed my options with other successful entrepreneurs, accountants, a few lawyers, and people within the publications industry.

At that time, the overall plan for bizMe was a printed magazine with new issues published every two months. So now add in discussions with printers and considerations for ads and postage and mailing lists and subscription fees. I was overloaded and overwhelmed. Without a Conde Nast, Time Inc. or Hearst Corporation backing this venture it was quickly apparent that a printed publication included way too many zeros in relationship to my limited funds! So I switched my thinking from a printed magazine to a web version. Online offered more viable options and the ability to fund it myself.

An excellent way to describe the business plan is as the blueprint of your business and the go-to plan to stay focused on how you want your business to grow. You use it as a reference to make sure that you are still on track to achieving what you had planned to achieve. I look at my business plan today and I am incredibly impressed by what we put together. Our research included hot careers for the upcoming college grads, how college seniors felt about entering the workplace — prepared or unprepared — and the reality of leaving the safety net of college and beginning a career position. We gathered much of this knowledge through a survey I created and polled with post-secondary students enrolled in business classes throughout the Minneapolis area. The entire plan was an awesome snapshot of our brand and the power it had . . . however, it is not even close to where our business is today!

The bizMe bizplan included:
Executive Summary
Company Description
Identifying the bizMe Buyer
bizMe Audience Analysis
Industry Analysis
bizMe Competition
Ad Rates
Strategic Position and Risk Analysis
bizMe Vision and Strategic Goals
bizMe Management and Organization
bizMe Editorial
bizMe Financial
bizMe Survey
Detailed Northwestern Mutual Millennium Study
Detailed Competitive Analysis
Facts and Supporting Data
Census Data Statistics
Media Kit

Recently I have been listening to audio books while working out which has been a wonderful way to get caught up on some of the great reads from my favorite authors, but also to hear the advice of business authors. I am so engaged by what I am hearing that I find myself running for an hour, which I never do! One of my favorites, Rework by Jason Fried and David Heinemeier Hansson includes a section on business plans. In their opinion, the "business plan is a waste of time because it is a) never looked at and b) isn't accurate or kept viable." Creating a business plan allowed me the time to really consider what I was getting into—I had the facts, I knew the financial considerations, I understood what I wanted for bizMe. So for me, the business plan was not a waste of time; however I do agree with the statement that developing a plan is time consuming and you may eventually outgrow the original concept. The business plan makes you think through your options and to weigh the "what if's."

Understanding how you want your business plan to work for you is going to determine how much time you want to spend on it. If you want to use it to find investors, then you definitely need a very thorough bizplan. If you are going to make your business work on the side while you work full-time then I would develop a plan that showcases the research, defines the mission, projects your vision statement and evaluates how your target demographic will benefit from your innovation. A well thought out plan will give you confidence moving forward and that is something we all need when starting our own business!

My quick thoughts on a business plan:

- A tremendous tool for organizing the structure of your business, defining the progress you plan to make and deciding how you will implement the steps to a successful venture.

- Initially, business plans were presented to investors but if you plan to boot strap your business, you may not need as much financial detail as when seeking angel investors or venture funding.

- Research, research, research!! This was my favorite part of putting together the bizplan. I knew before the idea of bizMe became reality that it was going to work because I had the research to back it up! Before you jump into any idea, put in the time to make sure your target demographic wants it. You have to know where you're going and why you're going there—that's the ultimate benefit of researching and planning.

- It helps you identify an exit strategy if you are thinking of selling the business some day or if, unfortunately, the business is not meeting expectations and you need to rethink your profitability and popularity.

- This last one is irony at its finest—don't obsess over your business plan but do sweat the details. The details I consider most relevant include:

  - Fine tuning your mission statement so that the identity and focus presents a clear vision on how you want your entrepreneurial venture perceived by the public.
  - Knowing your competition and being able to list why your version is more appealing, more streamlined, or more functional.
  - Understanding your target demographic as well as you know your family members. Your customer/client base represents an extension of your family—treat them well, offer a product that is irresistible, and you'll have them at first look!

- Be honest with your financial planning—have a solid grasp on the true expenses—how much can you invest without putting your personal finances in jeopardy? The first few years may mean many, many hours without a cent of profit. Are you financially, mentally and emotionally prepared for this?

A business plan is an action plan. Its Plan A and Plan B. It's the safety net, the oxygen tank, the exit plan. It's the key to success that you've mapped out so believe it, work it, and evolve it as your growth and success allows. After all, the business plan is the treasure map that you've created to finding your passion!

Chapter 5
Networking, smart schmoozing and working the room bizgal style!

It's all about who you know! How many times have we heard this but yet the idea of meeting people and putting ourselves out there to be rejected makes us shudder? I was definitely one of those people and truthfully I did not understand the concept of networking. I was under the impression that my business was like Field of Dreams. If I built it, they would come . . . well I can tell you, no one came. Day after day I was stalking my traffic on Google Analytics and noticing that only five people were going to the site per day and guess what . . . I had talked to five people that day. I did not understand how there could be millions of people in the world and only five people were visiting my site. What was going on? Most importantly, what was I missing in this world of RSS, optimization and web crawlers?

After a year of watching my traffic grow very slowly I decided it was time to jump in feet first and try this thing called networking that everyone had been encouraging me to do. I had been networking this entire time with all the informational interviews I was doing but the idea of walking into a room full of 200 people and starting up conversations terrified me. I can remember attending networking events, talking to one person and running out of the room, thinking to myself, thank goodness that is over. Networking is scary for everyone and until you force yourself to do it over and over again, it will never be comfortable for you. That is exactly what I did — I stepped out of my comfort zone and plunged in.

I know the power of word-of-mouth marketing and for a young entrepreneur with limited funds, this was the only way to build my business because word-of-mouth is free! We all love the word free! I continued to attend networking event after networking event because I wanted to be good at it. I wanted it to become natural and easy and eventually as I recognized more faces and names, it did! I fell in love with the idea of meeting others; sharing stories and helping others grow their success stories. I wanted to network every night. However, I noticed that even though I was networking all the time, my traffic was not growing.

I thought for sure I had mastered my elevator pitch, talked about what bizMe was and why they should visit the site. Would you go to the site if someone said this to you?

"Hi, my name is Amanda and I am the co-founder of an online magazine bizMe. bizMe coaches and mentors professional women on their career relationship dynamics, ethical values and overall career etiquette."

Probably not . . . and the reason is because in the course of the day, how many times are you told to like us on Facebook, find us on Twitter, visit our webpage, visit our YouTube channel (and the list goes on!) What makes my site different than anything else that is bidding for your time and eyeballs? It took me awhile to figure it out but once I did, I created a whirlwind!

So what makes my site different? Quite simply . . . ME! I make my site different from everything else that is out there. My reason for doing this, and my passion are what makes bizMe tick. No matter how hard I fought for the site to not be about me, (after all, I didn't start bizMe to become notoriously infamous) there was an element of the site that HAD to be about me. It illustrates my passion, my love for challenging people to be the best they can be, my story of who I am and how this business came to be. I found that was the story that people wanted to hear, they didn't want another website to casually and impassively visit.

I revamped my elevator pitch. I worked on my personal branding of who I wanted to be in the community, what image the bizgal personified, and when I meet people for the first time, what lasting impression did I want to leave them with so that when we met again at a different event, I was that same spunky, professional, chic, trendy, savvy girl they met previously. As astrologists would suggest, the stars aligned and bizMe grew!

This was one of my first "hallelujah" moments— As I told my story people started to gravitate toward me, they wanted to learn from me, I was becoming the mentor I had always hoped I would be and I was starting to build relationships. The bizMe traffic grew tremendously and the more people I met, the more opportunities I received. Networking opens doors like you would never imagine and now my networking community includes a whole bunch of wonderfulness—the publisher of Sports Illustrated, CEO's, professional athletes, small business owners and everyone in between from high school students to retirees who are busy planning another career. Each one matters to me very significantly!

I started this chapter with, "it's all about who you know," but to really make networking work . . . it is all about who knows YOU!! Just remember this when you are networking. It is great to meet power players, but if they don't know who you are and you don't have a relationship with them . . . it doesn't matter.

My 10 best networking tips:

1. **Personal Branding:** Determining who you are and how you want to be perceived is what sets you apart in the business world. Once you have figured this out, be that person every single time you meet someone whether you have had a good day or a bad day. Never leave people confused about who you are.

2. **Elevator pitch:** This is your 30 seconds to pitch anyone why you do what you do. Your pitch should not just focus on the WHAT but the WHY what you do or what you are promoting is important to the person in front of you. Refrain from being the robot that routinely spews out what you do right on cue when you meet someone new. Be genuine, be sincere. Remember that elevator pitches continue to evolve with your career growth.

3. **Breaking In:** It is very intimidating walking into a room of unknowns so I like to pause before entering and observe the dynamic of the room. Determine which groups appear the most welcoming. Find someone who appears approachable and start a conversation. When joining a group, I approach the most dominant person in the group on the right side of his/her body. I single out the most dominant person because in that group, he/she is the most comfortable and is able to keep the conversation going. Once you approach this person, be sure to acknowledge everyone in the group and make everyone feel they are part of the conversation. Works like a charm.

4. **The sequence of meeting someone new:** Observing body language, asking questions to learn about their business—who they are, and why they do what they do is paramount to building a relationship. Bottom line is that everyone wants to be noticed, recognized and appreciated. Be sure to then divulge the same about yourself. This is the key to building relationships—sharing, honest interaction, and listening. A great beginning when starting a conversation is "Hi everyone, I'm Amanda, great to meet you . . . Have you been to this networking event before?" or I might lead with "Hi everyone, I'm Amanda. Happy Thursday! It's almost the weekend!"

5: **Subject Matter:** Easy conversation starters include the event you are attending, the weather, sports teams, weekend activities, concerts, movies and other events going on around your city. Stay away from topics that are politically charged and religiously motivated.

6: **Food:** A networking event is not dinner so please make sure you are not eating like it is. If you are coming from work, grab a couple food items and leave it at that. This event is about meeting people, growing your business, not a free dinner. It does not send a professional message when you approach someone carrying a plate full of pizza. I can't tell you the amount of people that I have seen load up their plate as if this is the first time they have eaten in days, leaving nothing for others. Not cool.

7. **Drinking:** Limit yourself to one or two drinks at the most and then switch to water or ginger ale (it looks like alcohol). This is not the place where you want to get even slightly

intoxicated . . . enough said. A refreshing drink to request is a vodka and water with three lemons—try it, you'll like it. Well maybe one more cliché—loose lips sink ships!

8: **Getting out:** The most uncomfortable part of networking is getting out of a conversation with someone. You should never talk to just one person all night long so when you feel the conversation is over, kindly say:

> "It was a pleasure to meet you Amanda and I have enjoyed our conversation. There are a couple more people I would like to meet tonight, so let's follow up with each other and schedule a one-on-one." Or if you don't want to learn more about their business just remark, "I have your card and will be in touch." Easy as that!

9. **Follow up:** At the end of the night, you should have a new stack of business cards. Send an email to everyone you met letting them know that you enjoyed learning about them and that you would like to meet for coffee. You should try to do this in the next several days following an event so you remain fresh in a person's mind. Don't let too much time pass.

10: **DON'T USE NETWORKING TO FIND DATES!** I know this sounds funny but it happens and it has happened to me. Networking is not the new match.com or plenty of fish—it is a professional event designed to help each other grow businesses, perhaps find a job and to meet professionals. There's the term—keep it professional!

CHAPTER 6
Picture them in their underwear?

Some people believe that leaders possess special talents and a unique personality that has enabled us to lead, to pursue our dreams and embrace things that others only dream of being able to accomplish. But you and I both know that there is no perfect person that is good at everything; he/she just doesn't exist. For many, it is easier to make excuses on why we can't be leaders than actually trying to lead and failing at it. Leaders become leaders by putting themselves in uncomfortable situations over and over again until they have mastered it. Example: We all have talents; however, we choose to capitalize on some more than others. Have you ever met someone that is incredibly good at sports but has never played an organized sport in his/her life? I know I have. The reason they never competed in sports is because they didn't take the opportunities when presented. They were either focused on something else or it made them uncomfortable. This is the same thing with leaders. I definitely believe that all leaders share similar characteristics such as passion, drive, motivation, competitiveness, mental toughness, and the ability to accept negativity as an opportunity to grow.

    I am an example of a reluctant leader made into a role model/leader by putting myself in uncomfortable situations. If I asked the question, "Who likes to speak in public?" I would probably get very few hands in the air and I can tell you, a couple years ago, my hand would not be in the air either. The thought of standing in front of people and speaking professionally totally terrified me. Yes, speech class I could handle because we were all in the same boat and let's be honest, we didn't really listen to each other. I am referring to real public speaking—standing in front of people unknown, possibly with more experience and more knowledgeable and delivering a message in such a way that they walk out of the room considering me their new best friend, applying my message and changing their life. There's definitely an art to engaging an audience!

After I launched the first few issues of bizMe, I wondered how I could introduce bizMe to the college students in the Milwaukee area. There are several well-known women's colleges in Milwaukee, which made up my target audience within the immediate area. I wanted an opportunity to share bizMe with these students because the bizMe mission is to coach and mentor young professional women. So like I have always done, I picked up the phone and started calling the different career centers at all the local universities. Alverno College loved the bizMe content and asked if I would talk with their career development classes. Alverno wanted me to discuss everything that is in this book — the importance of internships, pursuing a career that fuels a passion, networking, becoming an entrepreneur and even all about me! How hard could this be? I know my story better than anyone

I remember the night before my first-ever speaking engagement and I was completely terrified. I don't believe I slept one wink. I was going over and over again what I wanted to say and how I wanted to say it. Thoughts about what could go wrong and whether the audience would be attentive or bored was spinning through my head. What if they laugh at me? What if I screw up? What if they don't like me? These are common questions and tend to hold most of us back from stepping out of our comfort zone.

There I was standing in front of 15 (yes 15) students shaking like a leaf. I have never been so nervous in my life. I don't think I said anything right or even made sense in what I was saying. I could not wait until my 30 minutes were up and I could get out of there! All I thought to myself was, "what a horrible experience and I am never doing this again," but by the time I got home from speaking that day I had several emails from students that had heard my presentation. Their comments were how inspirational I was and empowered they now were to go after their dreams. They really believed that if I could do it, so could they. I started to see value in what I could bring to other people's lives by sharing my story, but I wasn't comfortable doing it and I wanted to be. So I started speaking everywhere and I mean everywhere. I was that annoying person at Starbucks that would turn around to the person behind me and ask how your day was, I wanted to put myself into as many uncomfortable situations as I could. And so, I continued speaking—the more I did it, the more I loved it. I knew this was something that I wanted to do.

I developed a great relationship with Alverno and it just so happens that my friend who ran the Alverno College Career Center was on the board of the Wisconsin Private Colleges Career Consortium and she presented bizMe to the entire Consortium. That led me to present my story and career advice to student organizations and classes at Marquette University, Concordia University, Leaderfest, women's seminars and many more opportunities began opening up because people started talking about me!

When you become a public speaker, you keep your fingers crossed every time you speak that things run smoothly, the equipment is set up properly, the Wi-Fi works and most importantly that people show up! I have had my fair share of horrible presentations but the most embarrassing one that I am going to share with you occurred during this wonderful opportunity to speak at Leaderfest in Sheboygan, WI for one of the breakout sessions. I was discussing the importance of networking and how it can open doors for you. I am not a big fan of PowerPoint so you will rarely see me using it, as I prefer to include videos and social media. Well, in order to show video clips you must have the Internet! I set up for my presentation and I had my video clips opened and minimized. I was ready to go and as I watched the 100 people slowly start to take their seats, the nervousness settled in. I introduced myself, gave a brief overview of what I planned to discuss and was about to show my first video. I was so excited to show it because it was a clip from Ice Age when the characters are on this crazy rollercoaster slide. At first the characters were terrified of it but as they continued to go down the slide it became more comfortable and turned into a competition. This was a great example of how networking can be, terrifying at first but the longer you do it, the easier it becomes. Great idea, right? Well as I started the video, there was no sound and I tried absolutely everything in order to get it to work. Apparently we needed to set up different speakers in order for anyone to hear it. So my great idea backfired.

I decided to walk them through the video because I knew what was going on and what I wanted them to gain from watching it. This was only the start of a horrible presentation. I was all over the board in what I wanted to say and my entire presentation was off due to the video not working. I tried to hold it together as best as I could and when it was finally done, I was relieved. I was so embarrassed at how horribly the presentation went that I knew I would never be asked back again.

A few months later, I met with my friend who organized the event to hear her perspective of how it went. She brought along some of the Leaderfest participant surveys to share with me. I was so nervous to meet with her because I knew what she was going to say. . . that I was a major disappointment. I was actually shocked when she told me that I was everyone's favorite presenter of the day . . . WHAT?? That was unbelievable! She said that everyone loved how nothing I had planned to use worked but I held it together and got my point across.

The point of this is that no matter how uncomfortable something is at first, stick with it because you just never know where the opportunity could lead. A big part of my business now is motivational speaking—empowering my audience to be the best they can be. If I would have given up after that first class at Alverno College, I would never have received these amazing opportunities to grow my business, stretch my comfort zone, and discover a new passion.

Tips for when the microphone scares rather than engages:

- **So, the underwear thing** . . . not sure that works but whatever it takes, you must eliminate the fear of being in front. Olympic competitors love being in front so embrace that fear and use the added adrenaline to engage your audience.

- **The Intro.** True, everyone enjoys knowing that the presenter is a jokester but if that's not your personality then don't force it by leading with a funny comment. You never know whether it'll fall flat or have everyone rolling in the aisles. Perhaps you're a quote person and you lead with a dynamite motivational quote or a funny quip originated by someone else. Sometimes just acknowledging the wonderful group in front of you along with those that put together the event is enough to make the audience like you.

- **Know your stuff.** Remember, you're the expert, you've got info the audience wants to hear, so practice, and practice, and practice. Map it out — what's the order? Introduce segues or media clips that connect each topic to the next.

- **Energy.** That's the real key . . . remember the audience is sitting and listening — they're not active so you have to be the energy source in the room. Get away from the podium, walk around, make sure your voice carries enthusiasm and conveys passion.

- **Technology.** Whoa, it's either a home run or the worst unsettling nightmare ever in the world of presenting. Bring your own, rely on your laptop, ipad or flash drive — you know how your stuff works so use it.

- **Avoid another mundane PowerPoint.** Microsoft has created a tremendous tool but don't you think it's overused? Slides are not your crutch — rather, a slide should be used as a backdrop to your words, not the words of your entire presentation! There are some wonderful Web tools to discover—Prezi is a fun presentation program.

- **Disney has perfected the model of the guest experience.** It's all about the guests, the attendees, the listeners. So remember that word GUEST—and let it become your persona for presentation engagement! It's your mantra to be **G**racious, **U**nderstanding, **E**nergetic, **S**incere and **T**rustworthy.

- **Crave the spotlight.** At least for the time you're up in front. Think of how many people are, right at that moment, being impressed by your knowledge, how you carry yourself and how you interact. That's the impression that could mean business for you after the show! Extend an invitation for an exchange of business cards, to tweet what's happening and being discussed, to like your Facebook page. Before you know it, you've created a following!

Chapter 7
Putting a price tag on you

I wish every entrepreneurial encounter embraced the essence of mission and accomplishment. Unfortunately, for most start-ups in the entrepreneurial world, that is not our reality.

Our reality is more like hit and miss. Is it challenging to put oneself out there every day, meeting clients and seeking new business? Absolutely. I find that I am so pumped to meet with prospective clients only to become quickly deflated when the client admits to being just that lazy to enact any career behavior changes or when a client continuously presumes that knowledge shared is on a "pro bono" basis.

So how does an entrepreneur overcome this hurdle of offering a fair price for our ideas and experience? How do we put a price on our talents? Even established entrepreneurs encounter this pricing battle that we wage between what the consumer will pay and what we know our vision and wisdom is worth. It's a little different when your venture offers a tangible product but when your business is changing a lifestyle or upping someone's career game plan, how does one set a reasonable market value?

That's our daily dilemma.

Sometimes, the following has to be replayed over and over on repeat mode in your mind . . .

When you love engaging an audience and you know you do it well, it's not unrealistic to expect compensation.

When you provide a message to a packed-house audience that motivates and inspires and is attitude changing, it's not unrealistic to expect compensation.

When you recharge a client in a one-on-one session by offering solid, useable guidance, it's not unrealistic to expect compensation.

And finally, when you establish relationships with "movers and shakers" that others seek, it's not unrealistic to expect a good deed in return.

So, before I sound more like a preacher instilling a congregation on a Sunday morning or before you think I'm throwing a pity party, I'm just stating the reality of being an entrepreneur in an environment that is crowded with great ideas and visionary people.

Let's take a look at this economic principle of pricing from the viewpoint of a startup. Surprisingly, there's very little information available on how to price so I will share with you what I've learned. Just like the movie title . . . it's complicated!

And it's a lot of trial and error. And it's market demand and market influence—all that financial stuff you probably should have been listening to when in Econ class. One of those economic principles that should have been memorized is that customers and clients make choices based on getting the greatest benefit at the least cost. It's like the law of nature. Human Nature. And with that factor, comes the dreaded word.

Budget. Politicians fight over this word constantly. It's often an uphill battle for families as food and gas and recreational prices continue to escalate. It's tough for our retired generation as they stretch their pensions to meet living expenses. It's becoming an ugly word for our younger generation as the ramen noodle diet continues after college graduation because of the job market. So, it's a word that evokes a thousand emotions. And many times not the warm and fuzzy kind either! In fact, it's a scary word because it means failure or success. And that's the bottom line for any start-up.

And I believe it remains that way for any venture — and especially so for entrepreneurs. Do we devalue our services by setting too low of a price? Probably so in the very beginning as we fight to establish a client base. Do we overprice? Probably not because as startups we tend to be more sensitive to our gut reaction to fulfilling the needs of our client and tend to underprice if anything. It's finding that happy medium that well, makes everyone happy!

My best tips for establishing a fair price tag on you:

- **You're not a one-trick pony** so break down your services into categories and determine what you would be willing to pay if your income was x amount of dollars. Next, reconsider at another income.

- **Research** your area — what is the pricing for similar services? Are you offering more or less, not just in terms of pricing but in product or service?

- **Ask your mentors.** They know you best. They know what you can do. They know your end results.

- **Package your services.** Establish a sense of continuum so that clients see where you can take them. Offer a payment plan if that creates a more welcoming approach to growing your client base.

- **Be careful about undervaluing** — it can work against you. Inexpensive can mean cheap like in "you get what you pay for." Inexpensive may also "flag" you as inexperienced.

- **Deliver what you say you will.** There is nothing that will kill your image quicker than not being whom and what you say you are. Consistently live up to your branding. You want the public considering you as fair and ethical.

- **Leverage your pro bono activities, Part One.** This is a great way to build your network, show off what you're capable of, and support the events that matter to your community. People like to do business with those that have heart—that care about the issues and events that surround them. You cannot put a price tag on the benefits that come from volunteering and supporting others.

- **Leverage your pro bono activities, Part Two.** Ask for something in trade—a video of the presentation you gave, a review on your website, a list of emails of those that attended.

- **Don't give everything away at your initial meeting** with a client. Sometimes I get so wrapped up in ideas to get the prospective client moving in the right direction that my excitement becomes so contagious that I have already impressed, inspired and motivated a change after our first one-hour *free* session!

Chapter 8
Savvy Social Media

Scary thought for the people that are uninitiated to the world of social business: If you are not using social media everyday it is almost like you don't exist!!!

Way back in the day, businesses were built using word of mouth and grass root marketing methods. Today we have social media which I define as word of mouth on steroids. The intimidation of social media can overwhelm even the savviest of people but it is a band wagon that you need to get on and get on quickly! We have all heard of the usual suspects, Facebook, Twitter, LinkedIn, YouTube, and MySpace.

I know this may be hard to believe but when I went to college, we didn't even have Facebook. In fact, iTunes didn't exist either — we had Napster. I was driving my car when my best friend called right after we graduated from college and asked me if I knew about Facebook. I had received many requests to join but wasn't really into it. However, the more requests I received, the more I became intrigued.

Just like everyone, I began my intro to social media with baby steps — the simple process of creating a Facebook account. In an almost immediate wave of acceptances, I reconnected with all my friends. I liked the concept of Facebook because you were able to keep tabs on your friends without actually talking to them every day. However, Facebook is in constant update mode, which can make it overwhelming and frustrating for a business owner trying to leverage how to use it. At first it was create a profile to socialize. Then, create a group page for a business. So I created a group page even though I wasn't really sure what I was going to do with it, but I heard it was the thing to do. I invited all my friends and watched as my members grew. I was unclear where to go from there so I occasionally posted bizMe articles, but not consistently.

Then along came the Facebook Fan page! It wasn't enough to have a group page, now Facebook had escalated to fan pages. I researched this fan page idea and liked what I saw and created a bizMe fan page. I tried to get people to switch over from the group to the fan page, but let's be honest, that doesn't happen. So now I have my personal page, my group page, my fan page . . . and now Facebook has subscribers!

Social media has now evolved into social business which requires daily nurturing—posting, updating and being easily relatable to my readers and clients. I post articles not only from bizMe, but also from outside sources. I post quotes that inspire my thinking, activities I am doing, events I am attending and exciting news. All of a sudden people are coming up to me and telling me how exciting it is that my business is booming and things are taking off. In reality, I wasn't doing anything differently in my business except for frequent posts about bizMe on Facebook. What I was doing was making it easy for people to engage in my articles, start conversations, build relationships and I was taking bizMe to them! My audience didn't have to go to the website anymore if they wanted to read an article, I was making it easy. This is my point: If you are directly speaking to your audience and are constantly top of mind, you become a sensation!! It's that easy.

Now let's talk about one of the most misunderstood social media outlets—Twitter! It took me a long time to figure out how to use Twitter effectively. Twitter requires more of a strategy than posting on Facebook. Twitter is real-time conversations about everyday stuff and industry topics. When

I first started on Twitter, I wasn't sure what to say so I began posting everyday things like meetings I was having, outside activities I was doing (like going for a 2 mile run), and articles from bizMe. Nothing that I was posting was bringing any value to anyone else's life except my own. One of the challenges of being an athlete is that I like to compare myself to my competition and I was noticing that a couple people on Twitter were exploding with followers. That was not happening with my tweets. I started to study what they were posting, the conversations that they were sharing with others and the value that they were offering. Then I took a step back and thought about who I wanted to be on Twitter. If I wanted to be a career expert and someone that people looked up too, what type of information should I post that would ultimately be beneficial? I started posting articles about my industry, articles I had written, and I started to give other Twitter peeps the advice they were looking for regarding their careers. I was beginning to have meaningful conversations and people trusted my advice!

Twitter is a great tool to use if you are looking to establish yourself as an expert or the go-to person in your industry. You achieve this by participating in conversations specific to your industry by using different hash tags and following along in different Twitter chats. What is a Twitter chat? Great question . . .

A Twitter chat is a place where like-minded people gather on Twitter to talk about specific topics. For example: I started a Twitter chat with Manpower, a staffing company, whose corporate headquarters is located in Milwaukee. The chat is held every Tuesday from 12-1 CST and followers participate by using the hash tag #careerchat. I really enjoy moderating #careerchat and it has become very popular with job seekers, college students, career experts, HR people and recruiters. Every week we cover a different topic regarding career behavior and career advancement. I ask four questions or we have an open discussion so people can chat freely and take the conversations in different directions. By moderating a Twitter chat you are able to become the go-to person when people have career questions. I am trusted as an expert and I have developed relationships with people all over the world. The coolest thing is that I have garnered some really cool opportunities through Twitter. It is a fantastic social media tool!

Social Media has helped me take bizMe to a new level. Driven by the web and easily accessible on the smartphone and ipad, it's a "can't miss" phenomenon! If you want to build a business and you don't have the funds to hire a marketing firm, then this is the way to go!

Tips for using Social Media:

- If you are not on Facebook, Twitter or LinkedIn . . . you belong there! Hop Hop Dolly Dolly!

- Social Media is a tremendous tool when used correctly.

- Always bring value to the conversations you are having — know when self-promotion must take a back seat.

- Before you post anything, always think about what your boss, your clients, your followers will think about you as they read it.

- Keep all pictures and comments professional. No bashing, no bullying, no water cooler sarcasm when posting.

- Make sure you are checking your Facebook wall every day to clean up any comments that could make people question you, your ethics or your political viewpoints. Try to maintain a distance between the political climate and your own personal opinions.

- Social Media should not be used to vent your frustrations on your career, your boyfriend/girlfriend, your friends or anything else in your life. Everyone has down days; keep yours private.

- Social Media is not a popularity contest.

- Participate in Twitter chats that fit with your brand.

- Caution: What happens in Vegas, stays on Facebook!

LinkedIn Essentials:

- When using LinkedIn, complete your profile to 100%. This allows your profile to be searchable.

- The key: think like a recruiter in your field. Use the key terms throughout your profile that a recruiter would use to find you.

- Groups are a great way to start conversations with like-minded people and to stay current with the happenings in your industry. Join away!

- If you are looking to brand yourself as an expert, a great way to do this is with the Question and Answer section of LinkedIn. Believe me . . . it works.

- NEVER use social media as the new match.com. It is completely inappropriate to scour social media for dating prospects. Keep all contacts professional so your image remains just that — as a pro not a creeper!

Chapter 9
Being a Celebrity Branding Expert is Reality TV!

Mom knows best . . . yeah right . . . right?! Apparently my mom does know best because when I was younger she frequently suggested that I consider a career in broadcasting. That career wasn't even on my radar—I was convinced that sports management was my future. In fact, I refused to check out an auditioning opportunity with ESPN during AYOP (America's Youth On Parade, a national baton twirling competition) week on the Notre Dame campus when I was 15—ESPN was filming on campus and had a booth set up for would-be sports reporters to try out. I was an athlete with an abnormally intense interest in competition and training, but still scoffed at that broadcasting idea even with the camera crew within 10 feet of me! Ironically, I was interviewed at that same competition by the local newspaper and I thought that was cool! Lesson learned: Opportunity may knock, but you have to be open to answering! Today, I would embrace that opportunity whole-heartedly and would love to interview coaches and players along the sidelines or celebrities on the red carpet. I have found I enjoy spotlighting others and engaging in witty banter that showcases their cause, talent or personality.

It's remarkable that in one short year, I have been a guest on over 60 morning shows. Yes 60! I have no specialized media training, but what I do have is a tremendous passion for bizMe. That makes it easy to talk in front of an audience or camera crew without sweating buckets, or saying a bunch of ums to string together sentences. My attitude is my mission— to always present my career and lifestyle topics as a "just like you and me" conversation because that's how we learn best— from the wisdom and experience of our peers, colleagues and friends.

So, how did I land this great gig of morning show guest appearances?

At the beginning of 2010 I hired a PR specialist to brand the bizMe online magazine and myself as co-founder. Perhaps I set my expectations too high but I just wasn't seeing the overnight results I anticipated. We got a lot of media lists and we spent too much money sending out one press release that basically fizzled—no upswing in readership, no reporters calling for details, no reaction. It was like a slap in the face—the sting was personal, as bizMe is my passion. The harsh reality settled in that this branding of bizMe was ineffective and lacked the energy I wanted. I shy away from confrontation off the court but I knew I had to muster up the courage to have a "big girl talk" with my PR gal. I had to be honest and let her know that I was considering no longer moving forward with her.

Her response, however, moved her off the bench and back momentarily to being one of my key players! She mentioned she had a friend that worked closely with a TV station and she would ask the producers if they would be interested in having me on as a career expert. To cut to the chase—the answer was yes and I am forever grateful to NBC in Minneapolis. Although the PR rep and I are no longer working together, that relationship led to the beginning of my morning show appearances and I am thankful for her contribution to my career.

KARE 11 in Minneapolis was my very first morning show. We taped three segments for their Work It Wednesday features. I was so excited yet terrified all at the same time but once we got going, the anchor and I were like fast friends rather than meeting for the first time on camera! I took advantage of this awesome opportunity and told the anchor that I know content is the biggest priority and if there is anything I do have, it's definitely content. So I asked her if I could continue to pitch her ideas moving forward . . . hello Amanda the PR girl who toots her own horn and goodbye to those expensive media lists! I later read in a book that this was exactly what you were supposed to do. The best thing about working with KARE 11 is that we were able to tape five segments at a time so I was on regularly without having to travel to Minnesota every week. Worked perfectly!!

Getting my start with media appearances in the Milwaukee area market was a little different. I worked for the Milwaukee Journal Sentinel at the time and in our marketing department was a media guru. He had been a radio personality for many years and had a voice that was easily recognizable all around southeastern Wisconsin. I took him out for lunch and we strategized about marketing me as the bizgal to the media market in Milwaukee. He introduced me to the VP of Broadcast for Journal Communications. We had an awesome conversation and I was offering ideas left and right. I put everything on the table as you never know where it will take you or which idea will spark an interest. The VP then introduced me to the awesome producers and co-hosts of The Morning Blend. My first shows were round table discussions on a variety of topics and the Morning Blend team enjoyed my energy so much that I was invited to do my own career segments. During the summer months, I was on weekly! The co-hosts of The Morning Blend are some of the most fabulous ladies; they make you feel so comfortable that you forget you are on TV and not just at a Starbucks hanging out with your best friends.

Getting on the FOX Real Milwaukee morning show was a textbook case of, I know someone, who knows someone, who knows the producer! I messaged my friend who connected me to the in-between friend who sent me the producer's email. From there I sent pitches with talking points, suggestions for questions for the hosts to ask, along with the research to back everything up. The Real Milwaukee format includes four co-hosts and is more news driven than entertainment-driven. Real Milwaukee has been an awesome experience for me because not only have I made guest appearances as a career and image expert but I have also been invited to co-host many times. Co-hosting is the most fun and I love every second of it.

Connecting with Chicago's WGN and NBC 5 was all about leveraging my contacts because I knew someone who had appeared on each show and passed along the producer's name to me. I have not done anything unique or special to get on these TV shows besides pick up the phone, chat with the receptionist or producer's assistant and follow through with old fashioned gumption—plain and simple hard work. The secrets to being asked for a return appearance are to always be on time, to be prepared and professional and to have a lot and I mean a lot of fun with the hosts! If the hosts love you, you keep coming back!

TV is not for everyone, if you struggle with thinking fast on your feet and staying composed, then TV is not right for you. There have been several times where the hosts did not even cover any of my talking points and went completely in a new direction. Energy, enthusiasm, personality, and the ability to react quickly are the attributes that the media market seeks. You have to be able to go with it and still create good TV!

My 6 best tips for getting on TV:

1. **Pick up the phone and put yourself out there;** if you don't get an answer, keep calling! It is worth the extra minutes on your cell phone plan to reach someone on the phone.

2. **Content is king!** All producers are looking for solid content so if you have that, half your battle is done. Make it easy for the producers to pick you by sending them a solid pitch idea. The pitch format includes a few solid research or credible survey facts to back up your segment, what you plan to talk about, questions for the hosts to ask you, and the top three tips that serve as an action plan for your listeners.

3. **Play nice with others.** Anchors like to give their opinions on your topics as well so make sure you allow them to make comments. If you make the anchors look good, you look good!!

4. **Be Real.** TV producers don't want robots, they want experts that are real and who get it. If your industry has a lot of jargon that most people don't understand, don't go on TV and use those terms. Speak using language that everyone can understand.

5. **Provide viewer tips.** When you are deciding on a topic and talking points, incorporate at least three tips that people can

easily remember and you will become a media sensation because you have proven that you offer content and audience engagement.

6. **Look the part**. After all your efforts to get on TV, be sure that you now look the part! Sit up straight, understand the camera sequence, keep your hair away from your face and practice your delivery. Smile when you speak—you'll be a more engaging guest. Hide your nervousness with confidence!

Chapter 10
I always wanted a crown

Silly chapter title but oh so true! Even though I was a pretty good queen of the volleyball court, I always treasured the thought of wearing a sparkly crown on my head. Not necessarily a pageant title, but I wanted to be considered worthy of wearing a crown. Seems so hokey, but yet, I think we all want that heartfelt level of acceptance, that respectful praise for hey, you are good! and most importantly, the well-deserved recognition for hard work, persistence, and a heartfelt attitude. And to be honest, I loved the prizes and fame!!!

My world has always been consumed with ponytails, sweat pants, oversized t-shirts, Michael Jordan's, Asics, smelly kneepads, swamp ass, practices, games, training, lifting, eating whatever I wanted, setting team goals, achieving personal bests and doing it all over again. Female athletes are rarely described as glamorous or demure and quite frankly, if someone were to describe me as such, it would almost be insulting. As athletes we don't compare ourselves to other girls and think "oh look at how skinny that girl is or how pretty she is." Instead, we talk about how much weight we can lift or who we can outsprint. Our athletic realm is totally different because if I look in the mirror and see a lack of muscle, I freak out and hit the gym immediately so I can look buff again. Where I see muscle gain, other girls may look in the mirror and see weight gain.

However, let's fast forward to present day, seven years removed from my career as a D1 athlete. I still have the same competitive edge, the same mental toughness, the same body shape as an athlete but now I find myself a competitor in a very foreign-to-me environment. I have entered the stylized world of spray tans, fake eye lashes, hair extensions, dieting, photo shoots, fake body parts, standing in a perfect "S" when the cameras flash, and the endless over-analyzing of an everyday "look". No longer am I competing against athletes but now I'm up against former pageant contestants who have been in this type of training for a lifetime! And it's a tough learning curve trying to play catch-up!

About a year and a half ago I had the opportunity to do a morning show as a career coach/branding consultant (I started a reputation management firm.) Immediately I fell in love with the lights, the cameras, the on-air banter, the immediate give and take of live TV. I was a natural and truly enjoyed engaging the audience. I set my goal on being the best regional career/branding coach in the Midwest so as to catch the eye of the national market. After I have established myself as a savvy image/career consultant in the national broadcast arena, the ultimate goal is my own show on Bravo . . . how awesome would that be?!? Entering the lifestyle of wanting to be in the public eye, of opening myself up to a fishbowl existence is something I totally embrace. It's like being back on the court—anticipating the perfect set so that I can produce the pounding hit to outsmart the competition or gearing up for the stinging block that outsmarts the opponent. I love crowd approval and the roar of winning; the savvy camaraderie of being the best. I chase fame because that's what I do—I chase my dreams, I pursue my goals. So why do I want to be famous? Just the thought of being able to help others better their career life, to become more productive, more confident, more accepting of challenges and to have the security of knowing they can achieve lofty goals is what makes me tick. It's what excites me. I know I can inspire others—I've proven that when speaking on college campuses, in one-on-one conversations, and through my TV appearances.

So let's back up to the conflict of muscle fierceness vs. flawless persona—how do I balance the person that I have valued in the mirror for 30 years with the person that producers are expecting? I have always marched to the beat of my own drum and find a way to get things done without changing who I am; but I will admit, I find myself inquiring about hair extensions, fake eyelashes and the differences in spray tanning. So does this make me a sell out or am I playing the competitive game? Am I going to start a lettuce and water diet so I can be a size 2?

The only person holding you back in life is you. You will never be successful trying to be someone you are not; people can see right through that. I know I can make it in the industry without being a size 2 because there is a reason why I am where I am and getting opportunities. I know exactly who I am, where I want to go and how I want people to remember me and that has nothing to do with spray tans, skinniness or fake hair. However if you catch me wearing fake eyelashes, having a little bit fuller head of hair and a tan in the dead of winter, just remember, you can dress up a tomboy but you can never take the tomboy out of me. I am definitely not selling out, just playing the game!!

Your crowning achievement:

Strength vs. chink in your armor. Success is always built around strength. So find your strength. Simple route to success. I'm not referring to physical strength but to defining your passion. What is your intensity, that degree of force that provides your power and fuels your sense of accomplishment? Find that and you've find your crown.

Sweat vs. perfectly coiffed. Actually, sweat and getting dirty lead to discovering your level of persistence and perseverance. If you can tolerate the setbacks, the slamming of one door and the opening of another, the emotional toughness and self-reliance it takes to be your own boss then you've found your crown.

Starting vs. sitting the bench. You're responsible for understanding the playbook that gets you noticed. Know your competition; know what makes your intended audience or customer base tick; know your plan for winning and you'll own that crown!

Chapter 11
Toughen Up... thick skin is in!

Celebs listen up! Do you see the white flag waving? That's me . . . I am waving my white flag and surrendering my old thoughts. I was a believer that if you wanted to be in the "spotlight" you signed up for the negativity, the nasty words people would write about you, the constant daily judging because again . . . you "signed" up for that, this is what you wanted when you chose fame and being well known and easily recognized in the public eye.

Like many, I was "judging" a situation I knew nothing about, I had no idea what it feels like to be on TV every day and to have viewers criticize, berate, and analyze every thought and word you say along with whatever fashion choice you made to wear that day. Well I do now . . . !

I was honored with an opportunity of a lifetime—to fill in as a co-host on a popular Milwaukee morning show for three months while one of the co-hosts was on maternity leave. I was incredibly excited about this "big break" because #1 this chance doesn't happen every day and #2 I was given an opening to a field that totally fascinated me and in which I felt very comfortable.

This experience has been truly amazing, I have learned so much about the broadcast world, myself, the work involved in making an awesome show that keeps our viewers returning, the incredible team behind the broadcast, and what it takes to make it in this industry. For our morning show viewers, it may appear that our job is easy and that's our format—friends discussing what's going on locally and around the world. The four co-hosts sit around a table, chatting about topics and voicing our opinions. What people don't see is that we have already put in hours before the show, researching our individual topics and considering our fresh approach to the issues we plan to discuss. Then show time hits and you have to be "on" ready to discuss everything and anything that is thrown your way. Our show is unscripted so what you see on the air is all off the cuff as we have no idea what direction the other co-hosts are taking their topic. We respond to the energy and our own personal initial reaction to the others' topics. We have about five minutes to talk through each topic with a producer in our ear advising us when to wrap it up. To me, this is the easy part—doing the show and interacting with the other co-hosts; the hardest part is reading the awful comments written about you because you are the "new" person.

So, alligator it up! It's thick skin, sticks and stones time. Bullying is a very hot topic worldwide because of the devastating emotional impact it can have on children and teenagers. But rarely is it mentioned about the way adults bully each other. Perhaps it is perceived as acceptable because we are older and should be able to handle it and believe me, I can handle just about anything but some people can be just down right mean. We have taken a social media outlet and instead of using it for its intended purpose of staying connected to friends and sharing our daily life with others, we have turned it into an outlet where we feel we can say anything about anyone we want regardless of how hurtful or inaccurate or deceptive our words might be. And that's what this chapter is all about. Spreading the happy rather than smearing with unkind words.

As an entrepreneur my support system is often . . . me, myself and I. And when I get down, myself sometimes has a difficult time cheering up the me! Silly as that may have sounded, entrepreneurs are unique as they often run solo with no backup in front of them sprinkling fairy dust to pave their way. So how do you prepare yourself for when you hit the wall of negativity and disapproval? *Hint:* Under and around may take forever.

Up. That's the way. Kill 'em with Kindness is the outlook. And that's why you never hear rebuttal or retaliation from those in the limelight when untruths are printed or said about them. Success actually begins in the heart. What you speak and how you project your image all come back to what you have inside. You have to have heart, you have to have gumption, you have to have thick skin and you have to have the reasoning that can quickly erase the discouraging and detracting. Every motivational speaker stresses the vitality of positivism. I believe in the power of optimism with a side order of enthusiasm and confidence. That's what's in my heart.

What words got the almost-always upbeat bizgal down? Try these on . . . and I quote:
- We have no love for her. Depending on the subject matter anyone can be schooled. And she sure does not know how to dress. One more thing... Her better than everyone else personality mess up the dynamics of the show. You have 3 Awesome personalities then BAM.... Amanda. When she start talking it's like going to commercial. You check out of listing and do something else.

- lets start a facebook group to have amanda kicked off the show... who wants a boring blonde.... yawn :)
- Not sure why they keep Amanda.
- She sucks. You must be her mom.
- The perfect road trip would be as far away from that moron you hired as the fill in co-host
- It'll be nice when [the real co-host] comes back because whats her face is annoying as he%#! Sorry if that offends anyone...just keeping it 'real'.

Again, it's always perception. And my thick skin is reminding me that these are only 6 comments and the show has 35,000 viewers per day. So, percentage wise that's .00017143% and my feathers are ruffled?

Well, now I feel silly . . .!

My best tips for remaining positive, confident and optimistic:

- **Protein.** Wait, what? Yep, protein. Protein maintains strength, which promotes a positive outlook which guarantees that you are always at 100 percent of your game. And that's what gets you to the top and keeps you there. So check your diet and switch up what you're eating!

- **Be confident** in who you are and have a clear understanding that not everyone is going to like you. It's not personal; it is just the way it is. Chances are, the negativity is a sign of jealousy, lack of confidence or a form of flattery. Here's another way of looking at it—if they take the time to pay attention to what you are saying, you definitely have their attention.

- **My favorite quote** that I remind myself of often: "Judging a person does not define who they are . . . it defines who you are." ~ Unknown

- **Remember:** People do not control what you do or how you react . . . you are in charge of that. Keep your eye on the prize and realize that you are making your dreams happen and there is not enough negativity in the world that will make you stop chasing that dream.

- **Balance:** When you look good, you feel good and then you become unstoppable. The most important tip is to remember to take time during our crazy, hectic schedules for *you*. Make yourself a better person by working out, reading a book, volunteering, relaxing outside, whatever it is that you enjoy incorporate that in your daily routine. I love working out so I do that every day because it is my time to put everything down and focus on me.

Chapter 12
Leap Day... is Every Day

It's so hard to see oneself in a new role or expanding in a career direction that totally seems out of the realm of a self-conceived comfort zone. Deciding to write a book will definitely surprise my high school English and journalism teachers! Initially, when I decided to write a book, I felt completely overwhelmed by the process. How do you come up with a creative idea that is different, that people will want to read? How long should it be? In my mind, I'm much more comfortable speaking in front of a conventional audience than actually writing down words that anyone would want to read. What if I am not an interesting writer? All these questions were holding me back until I met with a friend of mine that has written several books and is incredibly successful. His words of wisdom . . . "Writing a book, Amanda, is all about telling your story. You know it better than anyone else in the world. Think about the question that everyone asks you and write about that." That proverbial light bulb looming over my head immediately snapped on as I thought about the question that everyone asks me . . . "How did you get started?" Then I realized that not only am I asked all the time to share my story (which I love telling) but that this is also the number one question that I ask everyone as well. I love hearing about how other businesses got started, the inspiration behind it and the lessons that are learned throughout the process. The reason all of us like that question is because no two answers are the same. Everyone has a different approach, a different system, different personalities and mentors surrounding them, a different way of how they came to find the success that they are enjoying.

As I look back on my life, I just cannot believe the opportunities that I have had. The ones I have embraced and the ones that I passed up. I live my life with no regrets. I reflect on what could have been, but never obsess on being regretful. We take the paths we do because we live our lives for us and no one else. I love who I am and there is nothing I would ever change about the path that I have taken and the fun thing is . . . I am only getting started! I am excited to share my life adventures, my ups and downs and my challenges with all of you and I hope you stick around because it is going to be one fun ride!

To close this last chapter of my first book, I want to recap the most important skills I have developed in the last four years of starting my business. All of these skills have been tested in person. They aren't things I have read or have been offered through words of wisdom. Every single tip I have listed are tips that I have learned by doing and I hope that you will use them in your own life's adventures where ever those may take you.

My 10 best tips that every bizgal and bizguy must know!!

You have to learn to hold on: Being an entrepreneur is an emotional rollercoaster. One day you wake up on top of the world, the next day you are questioning everything about yourself and your idea and wondering if it is even worth pursuing. If you hold on, I promise with every bad day there are about 20 good days following right behind. Persistence is the daily battle you will wage within yourself, but the benefit of seeing your dreams come true is awe inspiring and will lift your spirits way beyond any negativity or self-doubt you may have felt.

Just because you built it, does not mean they will come: I love the movie Field of Dreams. If they could build a baseball field and the ghosts started showing up. . . why couldn't I build a website and just have the traffic show up? Err, rewind—that only happens in fairy tales and movie scripts with happy endings! Things do not just fall in your lap in the real world, YOU are the controller of your own destiny and YOU have to be the one to make things happen!

You are as successful as the people you surround yourself with: Building a community of people around you is so very important because they become advocates for you. Just be sure to surround yourself with the right people—those that believe in your mission and vision, who respect your work ethic, and who speak the truth—not people who just tell you what you want to hear.

You are in control of how others perceive you: Knowing who you are and the person you want to be is what makes you successful. You control what others think of you by the way you conduct yourself, your attitude, your appearance and by what you say. Make sure you are always thinking—"if I met someone for the first time, how would I want him or her describing me or remembering me as I walked away?"

Don't obsess over your competition: I am constantly finding other young professionals doing what I am doing and it seems like they are miles ahead of where I am. I wonder all the time what they are doing differently, how they have more media appearances, more speaking engagements, or more traffic. I AM MY BIGGEST COMPETITION because I let this stuff cloud my head instead of staying focused and realizing that patience and perseverance pay off.

If I want people to take a chance on me, then I need to take a chance on myself: You don't need to quit your full-time job to follow your dreams. I was doing both for four years while I grew bizMe. However, you will get to a point where you are going to have to take that leap and when you do . . . it is awesome! I finally quit my full-time gig after four years.

Perception is reality: I remember when I started posting more articles and successes on Facebook, people started to notice how much bizMe was growing. Our site has over 350 articles and I showcase them one by one on Facebook. This strategy has grown our traffic because we are taking our articles to our readers rather than having them visit us.

You can only be good at so many things: I carry a notebook full of ideas that I have for future businesses; the key word is future. Don't throw yourself in too many directions because you end up doing nothing well instead of doing everything well. You are going to get many opportunities but remember to stay true to your brand and mission.

We create our own glass ceiling: Don't ever under estimate what your time and expertise is worth. Be confident in the product you are selling and what it is worth. Never, Never NEVER undervalue you.

Speak up or forever hold your peace: People are not mind readers and if you want something from someone, then you have to ask for it. People don't magically know that you are looking for financing, new clients or a venue to sponsor an event. If you need help, speak up!

There is not a single day that goes by where I am not thanking my lucky stars for all the people in my life, the opportunities I have had and everything that is to come. Remember you can never create your empire alone; you build it with others by being honest, genuine, sincere and passionate about what you do! I am so excited to be able to share my business with each and every one of you every day!

Chapter 13
VIP Shoutouts
My Very Important People

Alyssa Knier O'Brien

Alyssa O'Brien, DC owns and operates Align Chiropractic in Neenah, WI. She is passionate about educating her patients about the natural benefits of chiropractic care and helping them achieve maximum health and wellness for life. She completed her undergrad degree in behavioral neuroscience at the University of St. Thomas in St. Paul, MN. She then obtained her Doctorate of Chiropractic at Northwestern Health Sciences University. Dr. O'Brien has a passion for helping people of all ages and has completed extra studies in pediatrics. Over the last four years she has helped people with many symptoms, from infants with ear infections to elderly with severe degeneration in their spine. She also has a fitness center extension onto her clinic offering yoga and lifestyle classes.

My favorite memory of Amanda and I is that we continuously get overexcited for any big event and with that excitement, we stay up way too late dancing the night before. This excitement- fueled dancing always involves a lot of jumping, resulting in sore calves. If my calves are sore for a big event, chances are I was with Amanda the night before.

From the very moment I met Alyssa, I knew we would be friends for life, no matter where life took us. She is one of those very special people that you want to be around all the time. Alyssa and I have shared so many amazing memories together and picking just one is impossible. We have vacationed together, went clubbing at 4 am in the morning, bungeed jumped together, attended American Idol concerts, painted multiple towns red, caused a lot of trouble, broke a ton of hearts, cried many tears together and most importantly she honored me with the opportunity to speak at her wedding. I love you Alyssa and thank you forever for all your support.

Amy Fritz

Amy Fritz is COO at Fritz Inc. with responsibility for the tactical execution that keeps the household running on a day-to-day basis. She also serves as the CFO where she is responsible for proper financial practices and effective financial planning to meet short- and long-term family goals. Prior to her position at Fritz Inc., Amy worked in higher education. Notable is her six years at Alverno College as Career Lab Manager/Career Counselor. Amy holds a B.A. in Professional Communication from Alverno College and an M.S. in Administrative Leadership in Adult Education from the University of Wisconsin-Milwaukee. In her spare time, Amy enjoys reading, weight lifting, swimming, cooking, advocating for abused and neglected animals, and spending time with family and friends.

I had the pleasure of meeting Amanda several years ago when she contacted me about bizMe. At the time, I worked at Alverno College coordinating the Pre-Professional Seminar (PPS) course, a curriculum requirement for most students. I invited her to speak to all PPS students, so she could share bizMe with them and show them what a valuable resource it was to them as students and future professionals. As a result of many semesters of presentations, my relationship with Amanda evolved into a business friendship. I am inspired by her enthusiasm, encouraged by her success, and just proud to know her!

I met Amy when I first launched bizMe.biz, the online magazine. At that time, Amy was the career director at Milwaukee's prestigious women's college, Alverno College. I can remember the day that I introduced myself to her and she gave me one of the greatest opportunities . . . speaking! She changed my life forever the day she answered the phone and invited me to speak in front of her students. Sharing my story and empowering other people to go after their dreams is the unforgettable door Amy opened for me. Since that day, my career took a new direction and I cannot thank her enough for that!!

Chris Sherman

I am a father of two beautiful, adopted children and a husband to my hero, my amazing and very supportive wife. I own AmeriSign & Graphics, a full-service commercial printing and sign company. We offer products ranging from business cards, brochures, and pocket folders, to vehicle wraps, wall murals, structural signs and custom metal work. Creating something beautiful is my passion and I have found it key to surround myself with amazing staff who share that same passion.

Website
www.AmeriSignGFX.com

Work Collaboration

Amanda and I have worked together on various projects over the years and we both look to each other for advice in our respective fields. Amanda has assisted me with interviewing potential employees for my company and she has also been instrumental in helping me with some of my current staff members as well. She is a wealth of knowledge and her advice is always taken to the highest regard. I look to Amanda for advice and help on a continuing basis and she is always there for me.

I am such a huge fan of Chris and cannot sing his praises enough. He has been such a tremendous friend and has believed in me from the very beginning. His passion for his business is seen in everything he does. He pays attention to the details, he is trustworthy and most importantly he treats each client as if that client is his biggest one. I hope I can be the type of business owner that Chris is.

Daley Debutantes Baton and Drum Corps

The Daley Debutantes are a World Champion baton and drum corps. The group is comprised of over 100 members from Milwaukee and many surrounding suburbs. The group performs in numerous parades through the year. The Daley Debs compete each summer at the University of Notre Dame for the National and World Championships. The group has won both titles for 11 consecutive years. The group has performed in Ireland, Chicago, and at numerous college football bowl games.

Mission

The mission of the group is to give young people an opportunity to share their talents, learn to work as a team, and have a lot of fun.

The Daley Debutantes Baton & Drum Corps' tradition of excellence began when the Corps was founded by Sherry Daley Jung at age 15 and marched in its first parade in 1955. Over a period of years, the Daley Sisters won 65 state and national majorette championships in contests from coast to coast. From early childhood through college graduation, they were professional entertainers, appearing at conventions, dinners, sports shows, community celebrations, theaters, and supper clubs. They "grew up" on Wisconsin's first television station as regular staff performers on Milwaukee's WTMJ-TV and also appeared on national television shows such as Ed Sullivan, Laraine Day-Leo Durocher, and Ted Mack. Now in its 57th year, the Daley Debutantes Baton & Drum Corps has created an incredible legacy of excellence and status as one of the premier Baton and Drum Corps in the world.

Amanda is driven to achieve excellence in all that she does. She understands how much work is necessary to reach high goals and is willing to do it. She is a great team player and a natural leader. Using those leadership skills to help those around her grow and succeed comes easily to Amanda. She's also got "sparkle" which is why we chose her to be an Assistant Corps Captain for our Daley Debutantes Baton and Drum Corps.

> People always ask me where my motivation and passion comes from and I say the same thing every time . . . The Daley Debutantes. I could go on for days about how the Daley Debs has influenced my life. Sherry, Marcy and Patti have truly shaped me into the person that I am today. The Corps through their leadership taught me discipline, poise, and the incredible value of professionalism in all that you undertake. They nurtured in all Corps members to always realize that dreams are attainable but you have to put in the work in order to achieve greatness. I am going to tell you a secret that is going to surprise many of you. Everyone talks about an adrenaline rush and often times there are many things in our life that can give us this, but the only adrenaline rush I ever experienced was walking onto that competition floor every year at Notre Dame for the national championship and having our captain yell "corps ten hut." There is no better feeling in the world than this exact moment. Before every competition we would always say a prayer and to this day, this prayer still reminds me that I can do anything!

Daley Debs Corps Prayer:

Thank you Lord for the togetherness and friendship we share, for the hardworking members of the Corps, and the Corps itself. Instill in us the true spirit of competition, taking the pain of losing and the joy of winning all with a smile. Remind us Lord, that by doing our very best at all times, we are a winning Corps.

St. Patrick – Pray for us

"Who's going to win . . . WE ARE!!"

Danny Clayton

I wanted to be in radio when I was 5 years old---got my first job at 15---and had a nice career of over 30 years before that industry hit choppy waters. Rather than moving, we chose to stay in town and I began to reinvent myself, taking a job at Journal Sentinel in marketing. It was hard but I learned a ton. From there, I moved to Entertainment Management at a new spin-off company where we're investing in musicians with an eye towards performing and songwriting success.

I met Amanda at Milwaukee Journal Sentinel where she was a selling machine. I didn't see her a lot; she was usually on the streets drumming up business, but when we finally got a chance to talk things just clicked. I was amazed at her clear vision and supreme confidence—not just for herself but for the businesses she was dreaming up. I have to say, to see her jump from a well-paying job into the entrepreneurial jungle was pretty impressive but she hasn't looked back. I track her via social media now and see she's on TV, radio and now an author. I used to joke, please remember me when you're famous. It's not really a joke anymore.

I truly would not have had the opportunities I have had in the media world without Danny. Danny is the most caring, giving, self-less person I have ever met and I am honored to call him not only a great mentor but an awesome friend. He has opened so many doors for me and gave me the opportunity to shine by mentoring me and also introducing me to his network. When you hear Danny's voice come over the radio whether doing a commercial or a voice over, it is infectious and distinguished. Danny will always hold a very special place in my heart because he helped to create Amanda the bizgal!!

Frank Wall

Frank Wall is the current VP/Publisher of Sports Illustrated. He was a graduate of Indiana University Bloomington. His entire career has been in the media industry working for different media groups and now Time Inc.

Frank was one of the first people I networked with when I lived in Chicago. He worked for a national magazine and once I met him, I became an immediate fan of his! Frank is the type of person that you know the minute you meet him, he is going places. It has been so much fun watching Frank take on the Time world. He started out as an account executive for Time Magazine, then the Los Angeles Advertising Manager, Group Sales Director for TIME/Fortune Money Group, publisher of Money Magazine and now VP/Publisher of Sports Illustrated!! I am so incredibly proud of Frank for everything he has accomplished and I cherish our friendship.

Jane Guralski

Jane Guralski loves being a mom. But she also balances a busy professional life too--bizMe editor at night, secondary business education teacher and yearbook advisor by day. She earned her Master's Degree in Education and has been influential in designing curriculum, advising award-winning yearbook staffs, and making each one of her students feel like family. There's an art to engaging high school students and that is Jane's strength—creating creative curriculum that challenges, inspires achievement, and makes each day a fun learning adventure!

Working with Amanda has been an incredible insight into maturity, commonality, and sharing. When we began bizMe several years ago, I took on the leadership role—designing the website, determining editorial, selecting the writers. As bizMe has progressed, Amanda has become the face of our company—she is the networker, the social media expert, the on-air TV career expert, the bizMe bizgal! I like to think I have mentored her into this role, but truthfully, we have learned from each other and Amanda has blossomed into a fantastic entrepreneur who isn't timid in reaching her goals, who understands that image branding and persona is vital 24/7, and who makes everyone she meets feel as if they are the most important person. All of these attributes are instinctive and intuitive. I have total confidence that the bizgal will influence this generation and the next and the next and the . . .

Amanda charms my life and I love her dearly.

Behind every successful person, there is an even more successful person that just makes the other person look that good! My mom, who I call Jazzy, is that person for me. She is my voice, my backbone, my values, my personality, my strongest supporter, my success, my best friend and also the best Jazzy in the entire world. I know we all feel that way about our mom's and we should but mine is pretty tough to beat. I could write an entire book about what my mom means to me and how influential she is but I don't think even that book could signify the gratitude and love I have for her. I love you so much Jazzy!! Thank you for everything you have given me.

Jennifer Bartolotta

Jennifer Bartolotta made Milwaukee her home 9 years ago. Originally from Chicago, she is the wife of restaurateur, Joe Bartolotta.

Currently employed by the Bartolotta Restaurants as Director of Strategic Partnerships, she is responsible for managing the Bartolotta sales team who actively promote and sell the "Bartolotta Experience" at their five award-winning, fine-dining restaurants (Bacchus, A Bartolotta Restaurant; Bartolotta's Lake Park Bistro; Mr. B's, A Bartolotta Steakhouse, Ristorante Bartolotta and Harbor House) and The Rumpus Room – A Bartolotta Gastropub, as well as Bartolotta Catering and Events, with locations at Boerner Botanical Gardens, Pier Wisconsin and The Grain Exchange.

Additionally, Jennifer is President and Owner of Train-2-Gain, which develops professional socialization skills in employees, giving them the confidence to become ambassadors for their employers. Program participants gain valuable insight into the expected behavior of both their specific organization and the business world at large, and develop proficiencies to ensure that they positively reflect the corporate culture.

Jennifer believes in strengthening ties to one's community and, to that end, serves as:
Director, Care-a-lottas, The Bartolotta Restaurants Charitable Arm
Past President and Board Member, Meta House
President-elect and Board Member, TEMPO Milwaukee

Board Member, Wisconsin Humane Society
Secretary and Board Member, Schools that Can Milwaukee
Board Member, Aurora Health Care Foundation
Board Member, BizStarts
Raving fan, St. Marcus School

I had the good fortune of crossing paths with Amanda two years ago. I was captivated by her passion, enthusiasm, and sheer gutsy drive. Amanda's a contagious force of nature whose realistic approach to coaching is genuine, authentic and compelling.

Jennifer and I met through a friend and the minute I had her on the phone, I knew I wanted to be like her. She has an enviable business savvy that many men don't even have. She also has a no bs attitude and that is I why I love her so much. Our personalities of "tell me like it is" match up perfectly. She is the type of mentor that is consistently pushing you to stop making excuses and get it done. Every meeting that I have with her, I walk away feeling empowered to keep going, to continue to embrace all the challenges that are around me and to believe that I am doing the right things; it is just taking a LONG time! I cherish my relationship with Jennifer and I am very lucky to have her in my life. Thank you Jennifer for everything!

Joe Lynch

Joe Lynch is in his seventh year with Iowa State and third as a volunteer coach after serving as an assistant for four seasons. Lynch's primary responsibility is defensive training.

In Lynch's first six years, Iowa State established itself as one of the top defensive programs in the country.

Lynch came to the Cyclones as one of the most highly experienced club and prep coaches in the Midwest. The Wauwatosa, Wis., native had spent his career on the sidelines at the prep and club level, building some of the most successful high school and club teams in the state of Wisconsin following his successful playing career. His efforts have earned him national accolades as one of the most highly respected prep coaches.

Lynch affirmed his ability as a coach at the junior level and cemented his reputation as one of the finest prep coaches in the nation in 2005, when he was honored as the AVCA Prep Coach of the Year. His efforts brought national recognition to the ISU staff early in its tenure.

Lynch is an accomplished coach and player with over 20 seasons as head coach of several prominent high school and club teams in Wisconsin. He has two state titles and eight conference crowns as a head coach and has earned several honors as a player.

Lynch is the husband of ISU head coach Christy Johnson-Lynch. The couple resides in Ames and has one son, Jamison, and a daughter, Addison.

Probably the thing I remember most about Amanda was that she was always smiling and in a good mood. I am not sure why this also comes to mind but I do remember watching Amanda play softball and she was bored just watching dandelions fly around in the air not really paying attention to the softball game. I also remember having orange julius at your house for team meals.

> Every young athlete should have an opportunity to be coached by someone like Joe. He is a phenomenal coach that challenges his athletes every day to be their personal best but would also never let you get away with making excuses. Joe is the type of coach that you want to give 150% for because you know he is going to take you places. Joe coached me throughout my entire high school career and I can honestly say that Joe was incredibly influential in helping me get a full ride D1 scholarship to Villanova.

Kia Weller

A college girlfriend of Amanda's, Kia currently resides in Minneapolis, Minnesota where she is a marketing professional and yoga instructor. She is a graduate of the University of St. Thomas in St. Paul, Minnesota where she first met Amanda. Additionally, Kia holds a Master's Degree in Business Administration from the University of Minnesota's Carlson School of Management. She is grateful to live in her favorite city in the country where she has access to her passions — yoga, running, biking and spending summers at her cabin. Kia also has a love for traveling, dark chocolate and red wine. She has a dream to open her own yoga studio one day.

It's been an honor to support Amanda through realizing her dream to launch bizMe.biz and bizMe Consulting over the past ten years. I am grateful each and every day for her sharing her drive, passion and enthusiasm with me. Even more, I am inspired by her genuine character, beauty and sense of fashion.

Although I have numerous college memories with Amanda — including many nights of eating Papa John's Pizza on the dorm room floor, singing at the top of our lungs at a Britney Spears concert and our runs down Summit Avenue, most recently I took a mini vacation with her that I will forever remember. Amanda and I spent Memorial Day weekend in Savannah, GA and Charleston, SC where we had many long talks during walks on the beach and over fun dinners and drinks. And I will never forget our midnight crabbing adventure under Charleston's star-filled sky! It's true that friendships evolve as we move through new phases of our lives and this was a pivotal weekend that allowed us to grow closer, bringing our friendship to a new level. Thank you Amanda for being a constant reminder to never give up on following my dreams!

> Most of us have worked an on-campus job while in college and I worked in the phone center at University of St. Thomas calling alumni to solicit donations. The best part of working there was that I met one of my best friends. I remember the first time I met Kia—I even called my mom and said, I think I found my new best friend. Kia would do anything for anyone; she is genuine, thoughtful and incredibly fun. Over the years we have had some amazing memories together and I am excited for many more. One of the first gifts that Kia ever gave me still hangs next to my bed and I read it every night. It's become my mantra. Kia made it and the pictures of us look so young that it makes me smile. She probably doesn't even realize the power this saying has to my everyday life—

A strong woman works out every day to keep her body in shape...
But a woman of strength kneels in prayer to keep her soul in shape.

A strong woman isn't afraid of anything...
But a woman of strength shows courage in the midst of her fear.

A strong woman won't let anyone get the best of her...
But a woman of strength gives the best of herself to everyone.

A strong woman makes mistakes and avoids the same in the future...
A woman of strength realizes life's mistakes can also be God's blessings and capitalizes on them.

A strong woman walks sure footedly...
But a woman of strength knows God will catch her when she falls.

A strong woman wears the look of confidence on her face...
But a woman of strength wears grace.

A strong woman has faith that she is strong enough for the journey...
But a woman of strength has faith that it is in the journey that will make her strong.

~Unknown Author

Michael "Dr. Woody" Woodward, PhD

Website: www.DrWoody.com

Michael "Dr. Woody" Woodward, PhD is a CEC certified executive coach trained in organizational psychology and is author of The You Plan a book dedicated to career hunting in the New Economy. Dr. Woody is founder of the consulting firm Human Capital Integrated (HCI), a firm focused on management and leadership development.

Dr. Woody has appeared as a guest expert on Bravo Network's Tabatha's Salon Takeover and has appeared on Live with Regis & Kelly, FOX & Friends, FOX News, CNN International, Daytime, Better TV, CBS, WGN Midday, and WPIX New York. Dr. Woody also writes a weekly column featured on FOXBusiness.com called "The Career Hot Seat" and appears regularly with Jamie Colby on FOXNews.com Live to talk about workplace issues.

Prior to founding HCI, Dr. Woody served as a management/HR consultant for PricewaterhouseCoopers Consulting (PwC) and as a project manager for IBM Business Consulting Services. Dr. Woody also serves on the advisory board and as a faculty instructor for the Florida International University Center for Leadership.

Dr. Woody received a bachelor's in psychology from the University of Miami, a master's in industrial and organizational psychology from Springfield College, and a PhD in industrial and organizational psychology from Florida International University.

Contact Dr. Woody:
31 SE 5th Street, Suite 1201 Miami, FL 33131
Office: 305-200-5174
E-mail: DrWoody@DrWoody.com

I've had the pleasure of knowing Amanda for a little over a year and I feel as if I've known her for decades. Amanda's passion for helping others develop and grow is infectious. She brings a great energy both on and off camera and her Midwestern charm is irresistible! Every time I've left a meeting or finished a phone call with Amanda I've been inspired. Her unique perspective and original thinking have always served to spark my creativity and help me re-think my direction. Watching her grow as a career expert and media personality has been a delight. There is no doubt we will be working together in the future.

I am incredibly honored to have Dr. Woody in my life and from the moment I met him, I knew I would have a friend forever. It was friendship at first sight, but honestly it is hard to resist his charming personality. Dr. Woody has opened so many doors for me, that I will be forever grateful. People always say, find someone that you admire and model your behavior and actions after that person . . . Dr. Woody is that person for me!

My Family

There is a very special place in my heart for each and every one of you but the love and support that I get from my entire family every single day is what keeps me going. They have seen me on incredibly low days, high days, taking my frustration out on them for no reason days and everything in between but never once made me question whether or not I could do this. I often joke that I could have been a trust fund baby if my great grandfather would have made it through prohibition. He started an amazing brewery in Jefferson, WI right at the same time as Miller but the reality is, having a family bond in such a way that we would do anything for each other is priceless! Here is a huge shout out to: Jane, Virgil, SarahJane, Charley Guralski, Nana and Papa Heger, Ashley, Chad, and Leighton Smith, Bob Heger, Grandma and Grandpa Guralski, Mary Jo, Roy, Kirstie, Tommie, Maddie Overton. Thank you for everything!!

My mom and dad,
Jane and Virgil Guralski

My sisters
Ashley and
SarahJane

Phil Gerbyshak

Website: http://philgerbyshak.com

Phil Gerbyshak is the founder of the Make It Great! Institute, founded in 2006 to teach businesses and their organizations how to best use online technology to increase their bottom line, improve customer engagement, and increase employee loyalty. Additionally, Phil has written over 2500 articles and 3 books, his most recent book being #TwitterWorks, focusing on how small businesses and independent restaurants can use Twitter to effectively connect with their customers and potential customers. Phil has been interviewed to share his expertise in the Wall Street Journal, the Daily Globe and Mail, USA Today, CBS SmartPlanet and many other publications online and offline.

I've seen Amanda speak several times on panels with me about branding and social media. I've recently begun coaching her on getting her book done. Amanda, you've helped me gain clarity in my coaching and shown me that coaching is a valuable and wonderful thing.

Phil's smile and personality is infectious, he is one of those people that you could be around all day and he would have you smiling the entire time. Phil has been an inspiration from the beginning of this book. He has pushed me and challenged me throughout this entire process with a "get it done" attitude. When I first approached Phil for some help with my book, I was overwhelmed with the entire process. After one meeting, Phil helped me to clarify exactly what I wanted to write about and my chapter titles . . . his famous line "it's that easy." You would not be reading this book if it weren't for Phil and the encouragement he gave me every time I was held up on something. My favorite thing about Phil is his hugs, some people hug you because they think they have too but when Phil hugs someone . . . he really means it.

Tim Schlax

Tim Schlax is the Midwest Integrated Advertising Director of Time Magazine. In 2002, Tim was honored with the Britton Hadden Integrity Award, which is an award given to one member of the TIME community, business and editorial, for building relationships based on "respect, trust and honesty" with readers, advertisers and colleagues. It truly is a great honor to be recognized for representing those values.

Before TIME, Tim was Midwest Advertising Director of The National Sports Daily (1989-91), the launch at a national daily sports newspaper edited by legendary SI sports writer, Frank Deford. Before that, 6 years at Newsweek, 3 years at McCalls Magazine, 3 years at J. Walter Thompson Advertising as a media planner. He also worked at Leo Burnett Company in 1975 between his college years. Graduated Marquette University in 1977. Tim is also an avid runner with competing in 9 marathons all over the world.

Amanda has built something real, bizMe, from scratch requiring nurturing, relentless enthusiasm, energy, intelligence, marketing insight, style, good taste and decency; a reflection of herself.

Tim and I met a year after I graduated from college when I wanted to try the big city life and moved to Chicago. We met while I was doing an informational interview with him about national publications and we have been friends ever since. He opened so many doors for me when I had my dream of working for a national magazine. I was able to interview with the top magazines but I was never able to close. ☺ Tim has supported me from the beginning and has a very unique talent of being able to read me . . . which not many people can do. I cherish every lunch, dinner and our time together that Tim and I have shared. You are a great friend, mentor and supporter!!

And finally...

My goal is to empower as many lives as I can and although it may seem I am quite accomplished already, I know I am only hitting the surface. I hope my book *I am Not a Smartie Pants!*, describing how I have created my brand and the mountain of advice I have learned along the way has provided you with the motivation to follow what you love in all phases of your life—professional and personal. If you ask me about building success and what that looks like, I just might quote my favorite Chinese proverb: enough shovels of earth - a mountain; enough pails of water - a river.

People are so afraid of failing but truthfully no one actually knows what failure looks like. I have never failed at anything; sure situations have ended differently than what I expected but I would never consider that failure. A no is just a no for today, it doesn't have to be a no tomorrow.

Amanda the bizgal Career Store
www.thebizgal.biz

Speaking and Workshops with Amanda the bizgal

Amanda, the bizgal knows how to connect with an audience. The passion to inspire and empower is immediately apparent. Amanda absolutely loves engaging her listeners whether it's a peer-to-peer conversation or speaking to a myriad of diverse audiences. As an in-demand Gen Y expert and sought after image coach, her straightforward approach to today's hottest career topics offers a unique and fresh perspective that is relatable to every listener. As Amanda presents she relates on many levels—trusted best friend, encouraging career coach and influential role model. Always polished, Amanda will inspire your gathering of employees, conference attendees, or convention audience with real-life advice.

Favorite Audience Topics:
Andy Warhol is wrong . . .
Brand Me Beautiful
Generational Differences in the Workplace
The Business of Social Business
Using Social Media for Professional Development

Details available: www.thebizgal.biz

Consulting with Amanda the bizgal

Amanda the bizgal is your branding expert from initial bizplan to managing your own business. As a successful entrepreneur, Amanda is your perfect business mentor. She will guide you through those management and promotional details that take time away from what you love to do–focusing on your product, your service, your customers and being the expert in your field. The details that Amanda the bizgal can help you with to improve your customer base, polish your image and grow your social media presence: Personal Branding, Image Management, Marketing Materials, Social Media, Hiring Needs, Training of Employees, PR, Websites, Growing your business and Customer Service.

Details available: www.thebizgal.biz

Coaching with Amanda the bizgal

MVP Club Membership:

Join Amanda the bizgal and her expert friends every month as they dish on the topics important to you. You'll hear ideas that will influence your career, discussions that will become "aha" moments as you learn new tips to recharge your ambition and potential, and you'll love the opportunity to interact with Amanda the bizgal during the Q&A wrap-up at the end of each call. Monthly calls are an hour long with an open Q&A during the last 15 minutes. Each MVP club member will receive an MP3 of the call. Details will follow with MVP Club Membership.

VIP Club Membership

Everyone loves a little pampering, especially when it's VIP and there's no waiting in line! You're invited to become a member of Amanda the bizgal's VIP Club. You know you're a Very Important Person and a busy one too! Join Amanda the bizgal and her expert friends as they share suggestions to make your career and overall lifestyle more dynamic, more enjoyable, and more fulfilling.

VIP Membership includes 2 interactive phone calls per month. The first call is the MVP Club member call. Your next hour is all about you—your issues, your triumphs, your uncertainties. Amanda opens the lines to connect with you and you'll quickly discover a "just like you and me" friendship. You'll find the hour will fly by with tremendous sharing and advice. All VIP Club members will receive an MP3 of both calls so listening is at your convenience

Details available: **www.thebizgal.biz**

Amanda the bizgal 1 hour session

Amanda the bizgal is your perfect go-to partner when gearing up for your big "leap"! Contact Amanda the bizgal and get yourself in on one of the most productive hours you've had! She's immediately engaging and totally all about you!

Details available: **www.thebizgal.biz**

A NEW POINT OF VIEW: bizU

bizU is your virtual career center that extends the career services offered by colleges and universities through *just like you and me* conversations and webinars with Amanda the bizgal and her famed band of experts! Learn firsthand what recruiters are really looking for, effective networking skills that get you noticed, fashion sense that makes a lasting first impression, and most importantly, how to build dynamic career relationships and develop a personal brand that not only makes you highly marketable but gives you staying power. Additional content includes panel discussions from student leaders across the country along with a variety of career entrepreneurs from different industries.

Details available: **www.thebizgal.biz**

www.bizMe.biz

Amanda the bizgal's online magazine for the young professional offers the best professional and lifestyle advice in a straight-talk format. bizMe is your perfect coach—keeping you in the know on the hottest career trends to be your best and do your best.

Made in the USA
Monee, IL
09 December 2024